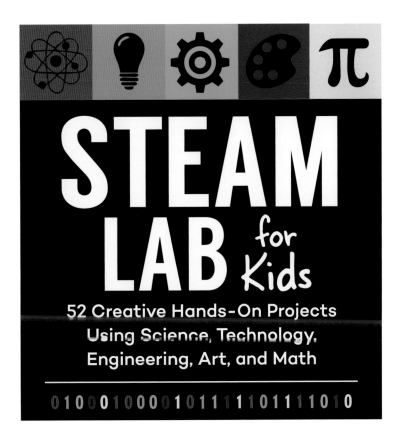

STEAM LAB for Kids

52 Creative Hands-On Projects Using Science, Technology, Engineering, Art, and Math

0100010001011110111010

LIZ LEE HEINECKE

QUARRY

Brimming with creative inspiration, how-to projects, and useful information to enrich your everyday life, Quarto Knows is a favorite destination for those pursuing their interests and passions. Visit our site and dig deeper with our books into your area of interest: Quarto Creates, Quarto Cooks, Quarto Homes, Quarto Lives, Quarto Drives, Quarto Explores, Quarto Gifts, or Quarto Kids.

First Published in 2018 by Quarry Books, an imprint of The Quarto Group, 100 Cummings Center, Suite 265-D, Beverly, MA 01915, USA.
T (978) 282-9590 F (978) 283-2742 QuartoKnows.com

Quarry Books titles are also available at discount for retail, wholesale, promotional, and bulk purchase. For details, contact the Special Sales Manager by email at specialsales@quarto.com or by mail at The Quarto Group, Attn: Special Sales Manager, 100 Cummings Center, Suite 265-D, Beverly, MA 01915, USA.

10 9 8

ISBN: 978-1-63159-419-9

Library of Congress Cataloging-in-Publication Data is available.

Design: Samantha J. Bednarek
Photography: Amber Procaccini Photography // www.aprocacciniphoto.com

Printed in China

This book is dedicated to
my dad, Ron Lee, who taught me
to love science.

CONTENTS

ENGINEERING

UNIT **03**

MATH

UNIT **05**

ART

UNIT **04**

FOREWORD

STEAM LAB FOR KIDS is the type of resource that no home, library, or camp should be without. Every adult who spends time around young learners knows the sound of restless footsteps, the fidgeting, hovering, and often slumped shoulders that all precede the question, "What can I do?" While many of us know these as the doorways to exploration and possibility, we don't all have the time or know-how to design the perfect experience. *STEAM Lab for Kids* improves every parent or educator's chance of capitalizing on "What can I do?" moments with over 50 well-curated projects that can help make downtime into "do" time.

The place for reframing how we introduce what STEM (science, technology, engineering, and math) looks and feels like is right at home. The value of the "A" in STEAM (art) is to help us realize the critical relationship between creativity and each of the subjects of STEM. Passing are the days where math and science are confined to sterile labs and classrooms. These subjects are alive, they're all around us, they express and emote, and they unfold in myriad and sometimes messy ways at the kitchen table. When STEM subjects emerge as expressions of our curious minds, the atmosphere is painted with enthusiasm and possibility. A STEAM approach encourages exploration and a new mindset about the upside of failure.

Adults take note: Supporting STEAM does not require you to be an expert. In fact, your learners may benefit even more from your willingness to learn together. Show them that learning is about taking risks, trying things, and diving back in when your first try breaks. *STEAM Lab for Kids* can easily become a guidebook for all to concepts and phenomena that adult learners might've missed the first time around.

My favorite parts of this book are the math projects in unit 5. The irony is that I'm one of those parents who could easily identify to their kids as "not a math person," but the real story is that I'm still learning and becoming the math person that traditional classroom approaches to math never afforded me.

One of the projects in the technology unit of the book originates from my learning design team at Mouse, where we are constantly testing experiences that close the gap between America's students and the leading edge of technology and engineering. We work to help a new generation to know STEM as a set of tools that can help each of us to express our ideas and improve our world.

I hope you enjoy digging into *STEAM Lab for Kids*. Resources like this one help all of us play a part in the high-stakes endeavor to engage a generation in their learning. Have fun!

—Marc Lesser, Senior Director of Learning Design, Mouse

INTRODUCTION

STEAM LAB FOR KIDS introduces 52 art-forward projects to help kids explore the relationship of science, technology, engineering, art, and math (STEAM).

While art is an emotional interpretation of what we experience, science is an analytical pursuit based on experimentation. Both are children of observation and go hand in hand with technology, math, and engineering. A group of artists called *the Cubists* didn't consider themselves mathematicians, but they created masterpieces of geometry by deconstructing and re-assembling familiar objects in new ways, allowing the viewer to observe a single object from many angles at the same time.

Ada Lovelace may have been inspired to see the future of computers as the result of her understanding of how looms create patterns in textiles. Louis Pasteur's love of art and experience in printmaking probably played an important role in his breakthrough ideas about mirror-image molecules, and Katherine G. Johnson applied mathematics to aerospace engineering to create a trajectory that carried the first humans safely to the moon.

While STEM education emphasizes critical thinking through problem solving using math and science as a basis for engineering and technology projects, *STEAM Lab for Kids* brings art into the equation—front and center.

Hands-on creative projects such as paper marbling help kids explore the concept of density. Colorful "stained glass" made from crushed hard candy teaches kids about melting temperatures. Cut up fruit is a hands-on way to learn about fractions and understand how the Ancient Greeks came up with the concept of the atom. *STEAM Lab for Kids* makes it easy for kids to explore technology by making simple robots, sewable circuits, and graphite drawings that carry enough current to light an LED.

This art-forward approach to STEM welcomes every kind of learner. Each project is designed to illuminate the concepts behind the fun in an engaging way that encourages young minds to pursue what interests them most. The labs can be done individually, in a classroom, or with friends and family. So put on some music, get out the paintbrushes, and charge full STEAM ahead into creative learning.

OVERVIEW

THIS BOOK PROVIDES 52 art-forward science, technology, engineering, art, and math (STEAM) projects perfect for countertops, desks, grass, and sidewalks.

Each lab contains an easy-to-understand explanation of The STEAM Behind the Fun to introduce vocabulary and other ideas related to the topic you're exploring. The labs are set up to make exploring STEAM as simple as following a recipe, with sections detailing the following:

→ **Materials:** lists all the ingredients you'll need to conduct each project

→ **Safety Tips and Hints:** provide common sense safety guidelines and hints for making things go smoothly

→ **Protocol:** (a scientific word for "instructions") takes you step by step through the lab basics

→ **Creative Enrichment:** gives you variations or ideas for taking the project a step or two further, ideally inspiring curiosity, invention, and problem-solving

→ **The STEAM Behind the Fun:** offers simple explanations and cross-disciplinary related topics

Whether you're exploring art or biology, experiences and ideas are made memorable by immersion. Kids should be encouraged to get their hands into a project, creating a physical connection. The processes of experimentation and invention are as important as the results, and it's essential to allow kids the freedom to dive in without fear of failure. Measuring, scooping, stirring, making mistakes, and troubleshooting should be part of every STEAM experience.

Many of these labs utilize items you probably have on hand, but the technology labs may require some advance planning. All of the supplies can be ordered online and most are relatively inexpensive. Duct tape, kitchen twine, a hot glue gun and glue sticks, rubber bands, paper, markers, paint, and glue will all come in handy. Tech projects may require small toy motors, alligator clip test leads, AA battery holders, battery snaps, and LEDs, so we've included a resources section in the back of the book to help you find what you need.

My kids and I have tested all these experiments, and they should work if you follow the protocol. However, at times, projects will require tweaking, practice, or innovation. Patience also comes in handy when you're learning to do something new. Don't be afraid to take things apart and start over. For example, if an LED isn't lighting up, you may have it hooked up backwards (see Lab 11, Light-Up Creature).

Remember, mistakes and troubleshooting are far more educational than perfection, and many scientific blunders have led to great discoveries.

UNIT 01

SCIENCE

ALTHOUGH CURIOUS MINDS HAVE BEEN ASKING QUESTIONS AND PURSUING KNOWLEDGE SINCE THE TIME OF ANCIENT CIVILIZATIONS, SCIENCE, AS WE KNOW IT TODAY, MOSTLY TOOK FORM IN THE SEVENTEENTH CENTURY. THE WORD SCIENTIST WAS COINED IN 1834. UNTIL THEN, PEOPLE WHO STUDIED NATURE AND HOW THINGS WORKED WERE CALLED "NATURAL PHILOSOPHERS" AND "CULTIVATORS OF SCIENCE," AMONG OTHER THINGS.

For a long time, science was mostly the pursuit of a very small group of people who had the time, opportunity, education, and money to do it. In England in the 1700s, wealthy families would invite friends over to observe scientific parlor tricks. Clergy, inventors, politicians, and writers gathered in coffee shops to talk about ideas they were experimenting with, and great discoveries were made in kitchen sinks.

Today, science is for everyone—and kitchen sinks are still a great place to start. To follow the scientific method, you simply have to ask a question, build a hypothesis, test your hypothesis, and draw a conclusion from the results. This unit is packed with experiments that explore the creative side of science. Scientists use models to illustrate how things work, and, as scientific knowledge advances, models are improved.

"I love neuroscience and theater because they ask the same questions: Why do we do what we do? What are we doing here? What is our relationship to each other, to this planet, to the universe? I decided to study both subjects to give them equal love and attention. I'm so glad I did because now I've created a career for myself that combines them in a fun, new way. By imagining possibilities and working hard to make them happen, I can bring something different to the table, a skill set unique to me that can make the world a better place and help answer some of those big questions."
—Sophie Shrand, science educator, comedian, actor, singer, and creator and host of Science With Sophie

CRUSHED CANDY STAINED GLASS

SAFETY TIPS AND HINTS

→ Adult supervision is required for this experiment. Melted candy is very hot and sticky and can cause burns.

→ Wear protective eyeware when hammering the candy.

→ Cookie cutters with simple shapes that sit flat on a baking sheet work best for this project.

Create gorgeous, edible art by melting hard candy.

Fig. 4: Bake the crushed candies until melted. Cool.

MATERIALS
→ Oven
→ Clear, colorful, hard candy
→ Small zippered plastic bags (1 bag for each color of candy)
→ 1 large zippered plastic bag
→ Protective glasses
→ Hammer
→ Baking sheet
→ Nonstick cooking spray
→ 5 to 10 cookie cutters

PROTOCOL
1. Preheat the oven to 350°F (180°C, or gas mark 4).

2. Unwrap the hard candy and sort it by color **(fig. 1)**.

3. Put each color of candy in its own small zippered plastic bag and seal the bags. Put all the small bags into one larger zippered bag. Seal the larger bag.

4. Put on your protective glasses and crush the candy with a hammer **(fig. 2)**.

5. Store the crushed candy in the freezer until you're ready to use it.

6. Coat a baking sheet with cooking spray.

7. Arrange the cookie cutters on the prepared baking sheet and spray them lightly with cooking spray.

8. Fill the cookie cutters with different colors of crushed candy until about ½ inch (1.5 cm) thick **(fig. 3)**.

Fig. 1: Sort your hard candy by color.

Fig. 2: Double bag the candy and crush it with a hammer.

Fig. 3: Add crushed candy to the cookie cutters.

Fig. 5: Remove the candy stained glass from the cookie cutters.

Fig. 6: Eat your creation.

9. Put the baking sheet in the oven for 5 minutes or until the candy melts and looks like stained glass **(fig. 4)**.

10. Remove the baking sheet from the oven and let the candy cool completely.

11. Carefully remove the candy stained glass from the cookie cutters **(fig. 5)**.

12. Eat your creation **(fig. 6)**.

CREATIVE ENRICHMENT

→ Try melting different kinds of candy to see what happens.

THE
STEAM
BEHIND THE FUN:

Most clear hard candy has what food scientists call a *glass structure*. Rather than individual sugar crystals like you see in table sugar and rock candy, it has a disorganized structure. When hard candy is made, corn syrup (glucose and fructose) is added to melted table sugar (sucrose) to keep sugar molecules from crystalizing. The long sugar chains in the corn syrup interfere with crystal formation, so hard candy remains clear and glasslike when it cools.

Stained glass art has been around since the Middle Ages. Unlike hard candy, real glass is made from silicon dioxide—the main component of sand.

LAB 2

HOMEMADE CHIA PETS

SAFETY TIPS AND HINTS

→ If you use regular clay for this project, it may fall apart if it gets wet **(fig. 1)**.

Fig. 1: You can use regular clay, but it may fall apart if it gets too wet.

Sculpt creatures with living "fur" to learn about plant germination.

Fig. 6: Watch the seeds sprout and grow.

MATERIALS

→ Sculpting clay or regular clay
→ 5 fluid ounce (150 ml) paper cups, one cup for each pet you want to make
→ Potting soil or dirt from a yard, garden, or park
→ Spoon
→ 1 teaspoon sproutable chia seeds (not irradiated)
→ Toothpick or fork

PROTOCOL

1. Shape sculpting clay around a paper cup **(fig. 2)**.

2. Use more clay to transform the cup into the shape of an animal, monster, or fantastical creature **(fig. 3)**.

3. Add soil to fill the chia pet so it's level with the top of the inner cup. (Make sure you have permission to dig, if you're not getting the soil from your own yard.)

4. Add the chia seeds to the dirt and mix them into the top of the soil using a toothpick or fork **(fig. 4)**.

5. Water the chia seeds until the dirt feels damp, but not soaked **(fig. 5)**.

6. Check the seeds every day and add water as needed to keep the soil damp **(fig. 6)**.

7. Draw a picture of your chia pet when the seeds have fully sprouted.

Fig. 2: Begin your creature by shaping sculpting clay around a paper cup.

Fig. 3: Transform the cup into an animal or other figure.

Fig. 4: Add chia seeds to the dirt.

Fig. 5: Water the chia seeds.

CREATIVE ENRICHMENT

→ Record how long it takes the seeds to sprout and measure how tall they get. Make a graph with days on the X-axis and sprout height on the Y-axis.
→ Create a larger piece of art using chia seeds and soil. You could incorporate recycling or create a design or maze using the seeds to create contrast between the brown soil and the green sprouts.

THE STEAM BEHIND THE FUN:

Chia seeds are quick-growing members of the mint family, called *Salvia hispanica*, hailing from Central and South America where they have served as a food source for humans for over one thousand years. They are full of protein, fiber, fatty acids, and chemicals called *antioxidants*.

Germination is the transformation from seed (or spore) to plant. When you give chia seeds the signals they need to sprout—water, light, warmth, and air—they grow very fast. You should see tiny white roots poking out in a few days, soon followed by a shoot and leaves.

Some artists incorporate living plants, fungi, and even microorganisms such as algae and bacteria into their work. Often, they use these living systems to make statements about growth, the environment, natural resources, the cycle of life, and decay.

LAB 3

CRYSTAL CREATURES

`0111010111101010101010101010010101111010101000000001000000001010111`

SAFETY TIPS AND HINTS

→ Young children should have adult supervision around hot liquids and Epsom salt.

Grow beautiful crystalline sculptures using pipe cleaners, Epsom salt, and water.

Fig. 5: Remove the crystal creature from the jar.

MATERIALS

→ Pipe cleaners (1 to 2 per creature)
→ 2 or 3 (5 to 10 ounce, or 150 to 285 ml) clear glass jars (if you don't have these, any size should work)
→ 3 cups (720 g) Epsom salt
→ Large pan or microwaveable container
→ Magnifying glass (optional)
→ 2 cups (475 ml) water
→ Food coloring (optional)
→ Pencil or wooden skewer

PROTOCOL

1. Twist the pipe cleaners into interesting shapes. Make sure they're small enough to fit into the jar **(fig. 1)**.

2. Pour the Epsom salt into a large pan or microwaveable container. Look at a few crystals under a magnifying glass. What do you see?

3. Add the water to the Epsom salt.

4. Heat and stir the solution in the microwave on high power or on the stovetop on high heat until the Epsom salt completely dissolves, about 2 to 3 minutes.

5. Remove from the microwave or stovetop and let the salt solution cool.

6. Pour the salt solution into the jars.

7. Add food coloring, if you want to (fig. 2).

Fig. 1: Twist the pipe cleaners into cool shapes.

Fig. 2: Dissolve the Epsom salt in water and add food coloring, if desired.

Fig. 3: Suspend your pipe cleaners in the salt solution.

Fig. 4: Let the crystals grow on the countertop overnight

8. Hang your pipe cleaner from a pencil or wooden skewer so it is suspended in the salt solution (**fig. 3**).

9. Let the crystals grow overnight (**fig. 4**).

10. Remove the crystal creature from the jar (**fig. 5**).

CREATIVE ENRICHMENT

→ Draw or photograph the crystals. Look at them under a magnifying glass.
→ Try to grow some Epsom salt crystals on another object, like an eggshell.

THE
STEAM
BEHIND THE FUN:

Epsomite is another name for Epsom salts. This useful mineral is made of magnesium sulfate and water and is used in both medicine and agriculture.

Adding lots of Epsom salt to water and heating it allows you to create what scientists call a supersaturated solution that holds far more dissolved salt than it normally would at room temperature. As the solution cools, some of the salt molecules stick to the pipe cleaner bristles. Other salt molecules start to snap onto to those molecules like puzzle pieces, creating the repeating three-dimensional patterns that form crystals. As more and more salt molecules snap on, the crystals become visible. You'll notice they all have the same shape, although their sizes may vary.

You can find gems and other crystals in art, including Chinese jade and the famous Fabergé eggs.

TIE-DYED FIDGET SPINNERS

SAFETY TIPS AND HINTS

→ This lab is not for recommended for kids under age 5.

→ Adult supervision is required when using super glue, sharp points, rubbing alcohol, and a glue gun.

→ If you add too much glue, the bearings will stick to the paper.

Make a super-cool spinning toy using skateboard bearings, Super Glue, and physics. Customize your design with a marker tie-dyed shoelace.

Fig. 4: Use a glue gun to attach the shoelace to the spinner.

MATERIALS

→ 4 skateboard bearings (available online or at a skateboard store)
→ Sheet of paper
→ Pencil
→ Ruler
→ Super Glue or Krazy Glue
→ 1 white shoelace
→ Permanent markers, like Sharpies, in different colors
→ Tray or colander
→ Rubbing alcohol (isopropanol)
→ Glue gun and glue sticks

PROTOCOL

1. Use a sharp point to remove the cover from one of skateboard bearings so you can see the ball bearings inside **(fig. 1)**.

2. On your paper, draw a 2⅓ x 2⅓ inch (6 x 6 cm) square with an X through it and put one of the bearings in the middle. Place the other 3 bearings in a circle around the one in thc middle so they're evenly spaced. Use a ruler to check your spacing **(fig. 2)**.

3. Add a single drop of Super Glue to the junction between each bearing to connect them. Let the glue dry.

4. Turn the spinner over and place another drop of glue at each junction.

5. When the glue is dry, prop the spinner up on its side and add glue to the junctions on each side.

6. Make dots with permanent markers on the shoelace.

Fig. 1: Remove the cover of the center bearing to expose the ball bearings inside.

Fig. 2: Center the bearings and Super Glue them together. Be careful not to get any glue onto the moving parts of the bearings.

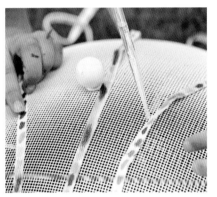

Fig. 3: Drip alcohol onto marker dots on the shoelace to create your design.

Fig. 5: Try your spinner.

7. In a well-ventilated area, suspend the shoelace over a tray or colander and drip rubbing alcohol onto it **(fig. 3)**. Dry completely.

8. Use the glue gun to attach the shoelace to the outside edges of the spinner. Fill in the gaps between the lace and bearings with hot glue **(fig. 4)**.

9. Spin away **(fig. 5)**!

CREATIVE ENRICHMENT

→ Find other objects that would work well to make a spinner with a skateboard bearing at its center. Can you cast your own spinner from hot glue (see Lab 34, page 96)?

THE
STEAM
BEHIND THE FUN:

If you look closely at a skateboard bearing, there are only a few ball bearings connecting the center and the outside part that spins. This means there's very little friction, or rubbing, between the parts. If you spin the toy around the center bearing, that bearing is called the axis of rotation.

The three bearings on the outside of the spinner provide the rotating mass that gives the toy a property called *angular momentum*, which keeps it spinning until the frictional force from the ball bearings in the center slows it down.

The pigments in permanent markers are trapped in ink compounds that won't dissolve in water. If you add a solvent, such as rubbing alcohol (isopropanol), it dissolves the ink. As the alcohol moves through the cloth you are decorating, it carries the pigments along with it.

LEMON-PAINTED EGGS

SAFETY TIPS AND HINTS

→ Adult supervision is required for chopping and boiling the cabbage and eggs.

Paint pink designs on cabbage-dyed eggs to learn about acid–base indicators.

Fig. 4: The acid in the lemon juice turns the cabbage juice dye pink!

MATERIALS

→ 1 red (purple) cabbage, halved
→ Large pot
→ Water
→ 12 eggs with white shells
→ Cotton swabs
→ Lemon juice or vinegar

PROTOCOL

1. Chop up ½ of a head of red cabbage and add it to a large pot **(fig. 1)**.

2. Add eggs to the cabbage and fill the pot with water until the cabbage and eggs are just covered **(fig. 2)**.

3. Bring the water to a boil over high heat. Cook the eggs and cabbage for 10 minutes, uncovered. Remove from the heat.

4. With a slotted spoon, remove the eggs from the purple cabbage juice and let them dry.

5. Return the eggs to the pot and let them soak in the juice. Repeat until the shells have a nice blue or purple color.

6. Dip a cotton swab in lemon juice or vinegar and use it to paint designs on the purple eggshells **(figs. 3 and 4)**.

7. Peel the eggs and eat your experiment **(fig. 5)**. Any leftover eggs can be refrigerated, unpeeled, for about 1 week to enjoy later.

Fig. 1: Cut up ½ of a head of red cabbage.

Fig. 2: To dye eggs, add white-shelled raw eggs to the red cabbage, add water, and boil.

Fig. 3: Use lemon juice on a cotton swab to paint designs on the eggs.

Fig. 5: Peel the egg and eat your experiment!

CREATIVE ENRICHMENT

→ Mix a spoonful of baking soda into a small cup of water and use a cotton swab to apply it to one of the purple eggs. What color does it turn?
→ Dye coffee filters in the leftover cabbage juice and use them as home-made litmus paper or draw designs on them using lemon juice.

THE
STEAM
BEHIND THE FUN:

Everything in our world is made of tiny pieces called *atoms*, and when atoms stick together, they create molecules. Pigments are molecules that give things color.

Red cabbage contains a pigment that looks purple in water, but turns pink or red if you add an acid, such as lemon juice or vinegar, to it. This happens because acid changes the shape of the pigment to make it absorb light differently.

If you add a base, such as baking soda, to red cabbage juice, the pigment changes shape again and looks green or blue. Scientists call pigments that change color depending on how acidic or basic their environments are *acid–base indicators*.

What kind of object, textile, painting, or sculpture could you design using color-changing pigments?

TABLETOP AQUATIC ECOSYSTEM

`0111010111101010101010100010011110101000000010000000010101111`

Create a self-contained living ecosystem in a jar.

Fig. 5: Enjoy!

SAFETY TIPS AND HINTS

→ Wear protective eyeware when making a hole in the jar lid.

→ Keep your aquatic ecosystem out of direct sunlight to prevent overgrowth of algae.

MATERIALS

→ Protective glasses
→ Hammer
→ Nail
→ Large glass jar with metal lid
→ Clean (rinsed) gravel (enough to cover the bottom of the jar and the roots of the plants, about 2 to 3 inches, or 5 to 7.5 cm)
→ Aquatic plants: Collect your own from a pond or buy some at a pet store. We used elodea pondweed, Java fern, Anacharis, Dwarf Anubias, Java moss, and moss ball.
→ Chlorine-free water (let water sit in a pitcher overnight or use bottled filtered water)
→ Aquatic snail (optional)
→ Aquatic shrimp (optional)
→ Algae pellets (for shrimp and snail)

PROTOCOL

1. Put on your protective glasses. Use a hammer and nail to make a hole in the jar's lid.

2. Add rinsed gravel to the bottom of the jar (**fig. 1**).

3. Add the aquatic plants, covering their roots with gravel so they'll be anchored when you add water (**fig. 2**).

4. Fill the jar with chlorine-free water. Re-anchor the plants in the gravel as needed (**fig. 3**).

5. Gently add the moss ball, snail, and shrimp to the water in the jar, if using (**fig. 4**).

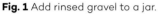
Fig. 1 Add rinsed gravel to a jar.

Fig. 2: Add your aquatic plants.

Fig. 3: Fill the jar with chlorine-free water.

Fig. 4: Gently add the snail and shrimp to the ecosystem.

6. Add 1 or 2 algae pellets and put the lid on the jar.

7. Enjoy your countertop aquatic ecosystem (**fig. 5**).

CREATIVE ENRICHMENT

→ Draw a diagram showing how nutrients and gases cycle through the aquatic system you created. Build a terrarium and draw a similar diagram. How do they compare?

→ Learn about the water cycle and write a story or draw a comic strip about a water molecule's journey around the world via the water cycle.

THE
STEAM
BEHIND THE FUN:

Much like your own school or neighborhood, ecosystems are communities. These complex, interconnected systems are made up of living organisms and nonliving components that cycle in harmony to create the delicate balance needed to sustain life.

Within the microsize system in this project, plants take in carbon dioxide and make enough oxygen to help the snail survive. The snail eats algae and produces organic (carbon-containing) waste, which fertilizes the plants, which make more oxygen, and so on.

Large ecosystems, such as the biosphere, consist of earth's crust, water, atmosphere, and every living thing. Water, elements, and gases cycle endlessly through physical systems and living things, maintaining the conditions required to sustain life on this beautiful planet.

WILDFLOWER PAPER

`01110101111001010100101010001011110101000000010000000010101111`

SAFETY TIPS AND HINTS

→ Adult supervision is required when using the blender and paper shredder.

→ Dry your wildflower paper immediately and do not seal it in plastic bags or it may sprout and mold.

Mix up some living paper using a blender, some paper, and a few seeds.

Fig. 4: Add extra seeds and petals for decoration.

MATERIALS

→ Shredded paper (inexpensive heavyweight construction paper, card stock, or watercolor paper works well)
→ Bowl
→ Water
→ Blender
→ Wildflower seeds, collected from outside or from a seed pack
→ 12 jar lids and screw bands from canning jars
→ Screen

→ Fresh flower petals, leaves, or fresh herbs (optional)
→ Hole puncher (optional)

PROTOCOL

1. Shred your paper by hand or use a paper shredder. Keep shredding until you have 4 cups (enough to fill 950 ml) of scraps.

2. Place the paper in a bowl, add enough water to cover it, and let it soak for 1 hour or more.

3. Put the soaked paper and some water in a blender and blend it to a fine pulp **(fig. 1)**. Add more water to the paper as needed while blending so the paper forms a wet, but not runny, mixture.

4. Stir in some of the wildflower seeds. Save a few for decoration **(fig. 2)**.

5. Arrange your jar lids on a screen, top down. Press the paper pulp into the lids to cover the screen **(fig. 3)**.

6. Add extra seeds and flower petals (if using) for decoration **(fig. 4)**.

Fig. 1: Blend soaked paper strips into a wet mixture.

Fig. 2: Stir in the wildflower seeds.

Fig. 3: Press the paper pulp with seeds into a jar lid on the screen.

Fig. 5: Watch your wildflowers grow!

7. Let the paper disks dry. Remove them from the jar lids.

8. Punch holes in the paper if you'd like to use them as gift tags.

9. Plant the disks by setting them in soil. Water them as needed and watch them grow (fig. 5).

CREATIVE ENRICHMENT
→ Fill in cookie cutters instead of jar lids to create interesting shapes.
→ Use wildflower paper to create living designs in a garden or container.

THE
STEAM
BEHIND THE FUN:

Seeds are dormant (sleeping), immature plants. Covered by a protective outer coat that helps keep them safe until they're ready to sprout, they're on the lookout for signs that it's time to grow. These signals include moisture, warmth, and sunlight.

Once a seed puts out its first root, it's stuck in one place. Luckily, seeds contain the nutrients needed to nourish the first shoots and leaves. When a plant starts to grow, the seed shrinks as the baby plant consumes the energy contained within it. With luck, the roots it sends out will find a good place to anchor the plant and find water and more nutrients.

The wildflower paper in this experiment protects the seeds and keeps them dry until you're ready to plant them. Then, it forms a nice foundation by holding in moisture and providing firm footing.

RAINBOW SLIME

SAFETY TIPS AND HINTS

→ Play with the slime, but don't eat it!

→ Adult supervision is required for this project.

Use glue and contact lens solution to create a palette of colorful slime.

Fig. 5: Store your slime covered.

MATERIALS

→ 1 (5 fluid ounce, or 150 ml) bottle of clear school glue (or white glue, if you can't find clear)
→ 6 small cups or jars
→ Baking soda
→ Food coloring in different colors
→ Contact lens solution containing boric acid or sodium borate
→ Craft sticks or plastic spoons

PROTOCOL

1. Divide the glue equally among the small cups or jars **(fig. 1)**.

2. Add a pinch of baking soda to each cup and stir to mix **(fig. 2)**.

3. Use food coloring to add color to each cup—yellow, orange, red, purple, blue, and green. Mix any colors you don't have: Blue mixed with yellow makes green; red mixed with blue creates purple.

4. Add a large squirt of contact lens solution to each cup and stir **(fig. 3)**.

5. Check the slime. If it is too sticky, add more contact lens solution and stir again until it feels squishy, but not sticky. You can pick it up and massage it with your fingers to help mix it better.

6. When your slime is ready, use it to create a rainbow **(fig. 4)**.

7. Store the slime in covered cups, jars, or zippered plastic bags **(fig. 5)**.

Fig. 1: Add glue to small containers.

Fig. 2: Stir in a pinch of baking soda and some food coloring.

Fig. 3: Add contact lens solution to each cup.

Fig. 4: Layer slime in a jar or create a rainbow.

THE STEAM BEHIND THE FUN:

Glue is a chemical called a *polymer*. Polymers are long chains of molecules. Normally, these chains can move past each other, which is why liquid glue can be poured out of one container and into another.

When you add contact lens solution to liquid glue, the boric acid in the solution combines with baking soda to make a chemical called *borate*. Borate is a special compound called a *crosslinker* that links all the long glue molecules together to create a big, slimy glob.

CREATIVE ENRICHMENT

→ Make more slime and create more colors by mixing different ratios of the primary colors—red, yellow, and blue. Add shaving cream or lotion to the slime to create new textures.

CONFETTI SNACK

`01110101111010101010101010010111101010000001000000010101111`

SAFETY TIPS AND HINTS

→ Adult supervision is required with the hot gelatin and agar mix. Make sure the gelatin and agar are cooled to a safe temperature before handing them to kids.

→ Keep the vegetable oil on ice as you create the agar confetti to avoid having to re-chill it frequently.

Learn how chefs create edible spheres when you try this tasty experiment.

Fig. 3: Drip the agar through ice-cold oil to make spheres.

MATERIALS

→ Tall jar filled to the top with vegetable oil
→ Gelatin dessert mix, like Jell-O (a light color works best)
→ 6 to 12 clear glass or plastic cups
→ Small saucepan or microwaveable bowl
→ ¼ cup (20 g) agar flakes (usually found in the Asian food section of a grocery store or online)
→ 2½ cups (570 ml) water
→ 1 cup (235 ml) full-fat coconut milk (not light)

→ ¼ cup (50 g) sugar
→ Squeeze bottles with caps
→ Food coloring
→ Medium bowl filled with ice
→ Slotted spoon

PROTOCOL

1. Put the jar with the vegetable oil in the freezer or in a bucket of ice to chill it until it is thick and ice cold, but not frozen solid.

2. Follow the directions on the gelatin dessert package for the speed-set method. When it cools to a safe temperature, pour most of it into the cups, filling each about halfway. Reserve about ½ cup (120 ml) in a microwavable container **(fig. 1)**.

3. Boil the agar flakes and water until the agar dissolves, stirring occasionally.

4. Stir in the coconut milk and sugar, mixing well.

5. Remove from the heat and let cool. Divide the mixture among the squeeze bottles. Color each batch with food coloring **(fig. 2)**.

Fig. 1: Mix up a batch of gelatin and reserve ½ cup (120 ml).

Fig. 2: Make the agar and coconut milk mixture. Transfer it to the squeeze bottles and color each batch with food coloring.

Fig. 4: Add the confetti spheres to the gelatin.

Fig. 5: Let it cool.

6. Place the jar with the cold oil in a bowl of ice or onto a flat surface. Slowly drip the coconut-agar mixture through the cold oil to create orbs **(fig. 3)**.

7. Using a slotted spoon, collect the orbs.

8. Rinse the confetti orbs with water and add some to each cup of gelatin dessert. Microwave the reserved gelatin and pour it over the orbs to trap them in the dessert **(fig. 4)**. Cool and enjoy **(fig. 5)**!

CREATIVE ENRICHMENT

→ Let one of the cups of confetti snacks dry out to see what happens.

THE
STEAM
BEHIND THE FUN:

Agar is a substance extracted from the cell walls of red algae. It's often used in cooking and science experiments and has a higher melting temperature than gelatin used to make desserts. So, if you put a piece of agar gel into melted gelatin, the agar won't melt unless the gelatin is really hot (about 150°F, or 66°C)! This allows you to create works of agar art in gelatin.

This project uses a technique called *oil spherification* to make agar decorations. Dripping the coconut-agar mixture through cold oil forms perfect spheres that solidify as they fall.

In labs, scientists use agar to make the nutritive substance used for growing microorganisms, since it won't melt at high temperatures in incubators. They also use it to make gels for electrophoresis, a process which electrically separates DNA and RNA molecules by size!

SWEET MOLECULES

`011101011110101010101010010111101010000000100000000010101111`

SAFETY TIPS AND HINTS

→ Young children should have adult supervision around candy that may be a choking hazard.

Use candy "atoms" to build model molecules you can eat.

Fig. 2: Use toothpicks to connect candy and create new molecules.

MATERIALS

→ Different colors and types of soft candy, such as gumdrops and gummy bears
→ Toothpicks
→ Wooden skewers (optional)
→ Apples (optional)

PROTOCOL

1. Look at illustrations in science books or on the internet of molecules like water, ammonia, carbon dioxide, benzene, and DNA.

2. Choose which candy will represent different atoms and molecules **(fig. 1)**.

3. Using the illustrations as guides, use toothpicks to connect the candies and create models of the molecules. One toothpick can represent a single bond, and two toothpicks can depict a double bond **(fig. 2)**. Choose a different color candy for each atom type you represent.

4. Large molecules can be assembled on skewers and anchored onto apples, if desired **(fig. 3)**.

5. How many kinds of molecules can you create **(figs. 4 and 5)**?

Fig. 1: Choose soft candy to represent atoms and molecules.

Fig. 3: Anchor large molecules using skewers.

Fig. 4: How many kinds of molecules can you make?

Fig. 5: Here's a candy DNA strand.

CREATIVE ENRICHMENT

→ Conduct some research on how water molecules interact with one another. Make lots of water molecule models from candy. Put them on a cookie sheet or large sheet of paper and assemble them to look like water vapor, then liquid water, and then ice. Take photos of each and compare.

THE
STEAM
BEHIND THE FUN:

Everything in our world is made of tiny pieces of matter called *atoms*. These atoms interact with each other and can form bonds with other atoms to create larger structures called *molecules*.

Although atoms and molecules are much too small to see with our naked eyes, scientists understand enough about them to predict how they might look if drawn on paper or modeled in three dimensions.

Our sense of touch gives us understanding and memory. Building molecular models, like the ones in this lab, allows us to get our hands onto a concept and understand it.

Perhaps that's why sculpture is such a moving art form. We can appreciate what sculptors are trying to communicate using our eyes, but we can also put our hands on their work.

UNIT 02

TECHNOLOGY

IN THE GREEK MYTH *PYGMALION*, A SCULPTOR CREATES A MARBLE STATUE, FALLS IN LOVE WITH IT, AND IT COMES TO LIFE. TODAY, THE MODERN WORLD IS IN LOVE WITH TECHNOLOGY AND THE INTERACTIVE DEVICES IT'S HELPED US CREATE.

In recent decades, we've brought ideas—that once seemed impossible—to life. Technology has improved our lives in many ways, but it is a medium that pushes back. Just as we've shaped technology, the products we've created have changed us and we continue to learn how to live with them.

Because technology is such an important part of our lives, it's essential to understand some of the basic science and engineering that makes the modern world tick. Most technology is powered by electricity, which can be used to run motors, power computers, and light LEDs (light-emitting diodes).

In this unit, the labs are opportunities to try your hand at using technology to assemble electrical circuits, light LEDs, play with solar cells, make motors spin, and build simple robots.

> *"Creativity and science connect the dots for the technology of tomorrow. Through a year and a half of hilarious trial and error, we created a violin that the world has never seen before. The Hovalin is a 3-D printable violin for nerds, by nerds. Creating it was a labor of love, requiring knowledge of software, violin techniques, 3-D design, and the ability to embrace failure."*
> *—Kaitlyn Hova, UX developer, neuroscientist, violinist/composer, and cofounder of Hova Labs*

LIGHT-UP CREATURE

SAFETY TIPS AND HINTS

→ Coin cell batteries and LEDs are choking hazards. Young children should have adult supervision when doing this activity.

→ **Short circuit warning!** Make sure the positive and negative legs of the LED don't touch each other! They should be completely separate. If they touch, it creates a *short circuit*, which will break the LED light!

You've seen light-emitting diodes (LEDs) in your smartphone as indicator lights, in streetlights, on a computer power button, and as lights on a microwave. In this experiment from the youth development nonprofit Mouse, we'll create an LED light-up creature to learn how simple circuits work. In this activity, you'll design a monster, animal, or any type of creature and make it light up by creating a circuit out of LED lights and tiny coin cell batteries. To learn more about Mouse, see page 141 or visit mouse.org.

Fig. 4: Tape the LEDs to the batteries.

MATERIALS

→ 2 LED lights
→ 2 (3 volt) coin cell batteries
→ Tape
→ 1 paper cup (something to make the body of the creature)

→ **Craft materials, for example:**
• Scissors
• Markers
• Construction paper
• Pipe cleaners
• Craft sticks
• Play clay
• Plastic forks or spoons

PROTOCOL

1. The 2 legs of your LED light are made of conductive metal and help you connect your LED light within the circuit. The **longer leg is positive (+)** and the **shorter end is negative (−) or "ground."**

2. Try to light your LED by touching the coin cell battery. The long LED leg needs to touch the positive side (+) of the battery, while the short LED leg needs to touch the negative (−) side of the battery **(fig. 1)**. If it didn't light, try again.

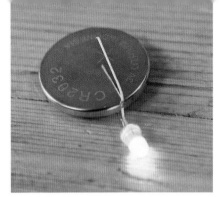
Fig. 1: Try to light your LED.

Fig. 2: Design and start building your creature.

Fig. 3: Make holes for the LEDS.

3. Design your creature: The creature you design will have at least 2 LED lights—the rest is up to you. Before you start building, what type of creature are you going to make? Make a sketch, if you like **(fig. 2)**.

4. Poke the legs of the LED lights through the cup where you want the lights to be. You can use scissors or a pencil to make the holes, if it helps **(fig. 3)**.

5 Place the LED's positive and negative legs on the matching sides of the battery and use tape to keep it in place. Place both of your LEDs this way **(fig. 4)**.

6. Use craft supplies or whatever you can find around your space to design your creature. Take a photo of your creature **(fig. 5)**.

Fig. 5: Be creative with your decorations!

THE
STEAM
BEHIND THE FUN:

A simple circuit has three parts connected in a circle: a power source, conductive material, and a load (the thing that consumes the power)—in this case, the light!

Your creature has a circuit for each LED light-battery combo. The positive and negative metal legs of the LED light connect the light and battery to each other and keep the electrons flowing in a circle.

CREATIVE ENRICHMENT

→ How would you get the LED to light up if the battery had to be placed 3 feet (1 m) away?
→ How many LED lights can you connect to 1 (3 volt) battery? Try it!

LAB 12

HOMEMADE DISCO BALL

0111010111101010101010100010111101010000000100000000101011111

Dance the night away under the swirling stars created by a disco light you built yourself.

Fig. 5: Enjoy the disco light!

SAFETY TIPS AND HINTS
→ Young children should have adult supervision around batteries.

MATERIALS
→ Glue
→ Sequins or large glitter
→ Styrofoam ball
→ Small low-speed DC (direct current) motor or gear motor
→ Battery snaps or alligator clip test leads
→ Tape
→ Flashlight
→ AA battery holder
→ 2 AA batteries

PROTOCOL
1. Use glue to cover a Styrofoam ball with sequins **(fig. 1)**.

2. Attach the ball to the rotating part of the gear motor. If you use glue, be careful not to glue any moving parts and only use a little bit, so you can remove the ball.

3. Attach the motor to a battery snap or alligator clip test leads.

4. Put the batteries in the battery holder and test the motor by clipping the snaps or alligator clips to the metal terminals of the battery holder **(fig. 2)**.

5. Tape the battery holder next to the motor under a countertop or onto a surface **(fig. 3)**.

6. Shine a flashlight on the disco ball from several angles to determine how you want to position it. Tape it into position using duct tape and turn it on **(figs. 3 and 4)**.

7. Attach the battery holder to the motor using the alligator clips and enjoy the show **(fig. 5)**.

Fig. 1: Glue sequins onto a foam ball.

Fig. 2: Attach the foam ball to a gear motor and hook the motor to a battery snap or alligator clip test leads.

Fig. 3: Determine where to position the flashlight.

Fig. 4: Duct tape everything into place.

CREATIVE ENRICHMENT

→ Make different sizes of disco balls to attach to the motor to see what happens.

→ Draw a light source in one corner of a piece of paper and an apple in the center of the page. Try to draw light beams from the light source to the apple to see where they would reflect. Where would the shadows fall? Try the same thing, but draw light rays hitting waves on a lake. How would you paint this? How does the time of day affect the light?

THE STEAM
BEHIND THE FUN:

Most objects don't give off their own light. Instead, they reflect, or scatter, light given off by other objects, such as the sun or a light bulb.

Imagine that a light ray hits a flat mirror. The light hits the surface at an angle, called the *angle of incidence*, and is reflected at an angle called the *angle of reflection*. It is reflected at exactly the same angle that it hit the surface, but is reflected on the opposite side of an imaginary plane that is perpendicular to the flat mirror.

Mirror balls have lots of reflective surfaces assembled at different angles, so when light hits them, the reflections go in all directions.

Artists spend a lot of time thinking about how to depict light in their art. Waves and moving water are especially tricky, as the result of constantly changing mirrorlike surfaces which create complex patterns of reflections.

SOLAR LIGHT FIREFLIES

Harness the Sun's energy to create glowing garden decorations.

Fig. 6: Watch your firefly light up when the sun goes down.

SAFETY TIPS AND HINTS

→ Adult supervision is required when using a glue gun.

MATERIALS

→ Small LED solar garden light
→ 1 or 2 sparkly pipe cleaners or a small piece of aluminum foil
→ Fishing line
→ Scissors
→ Glue gun and glue sticks

PROTOCOL

1. Remove the plastic cover from a garden solar light. Turn the solar light switch to ON, if it has one **(fig. 1)**.

2. Bend a piece of pipe cleaner or aluminum foil to make it look like a small firefly that will fit in the plastic part of the light. Attach it to some fishing line using a glue gun **(fig. 2)**.

3. Cut the fishing line to a length that will allow the attached firefly to dangle from a spot near the LED, down into the plastic chamber.

4. Attach the fishing line to the spot near the LED using the glue gun **(fig. 3)**. Reattach the cover.

5. Decorate the light and hang the firefly light from a tree branch or put it in a fairy garden **(fig. 4)**.

Fig. 1: Remove the plastic cover from a small solar garden light.

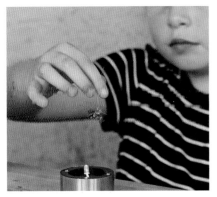

Fig. 2: Make a tiny firefly using a metallic pipe cleaner and attach it to fishing line.

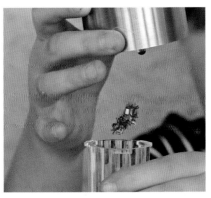

Fig. 3: Attach the fishing line to the light and reattach the cover.

Fig. 4: Decorate the light. Hang it from a tree branch or put it in a fairy garden.

Fig. 5: Find a sunny spot for your solar firefly.

6. Find a spot where it gets some sunlight during the day **(fig. 5)**.

7. Enjoy the glow when the sun goes down **(fig. 6)**.

CREATIVE ENRICHMENT

→ Create another project with a solar light. Can you design a light-up snow globe? Could you make another piece of garden art that is illuminated at night?

THE
STEAM
BEHIND THE FUN:

The Sun bathes the earth in energy. Almost all life depends on solar radiation to power photosynthesis, which sustains the food chain and adds oxygen to the atmosphere. Even fossil fuels contain the Sun's energy, trapped in the remains of plants and animals that lived millions of years ago.

Not only is the Sun's energy plentiful, it's free. The hard part about collecting solar energy is storing it for times when sunlight isn't readily available, like night.

Solar panels are made of sandwiches of materials that are good at moving electrons around. When sunlight hits these panels, electrons get knocked off and move from one layer to the other, creating electrical current that can be stored in a battery.

The battery in solar garden lights is turned on when the sun goes down and lights up the LED inside.

GRAPHITE CIRCUITS

0111010111110101010101010100010111101010100000001000000010101111

SAFETY TIPS AND HINTS

→ Adult supervision is required for this lab.

→ School pencils will not work well for this lab. Soft graphite pencils and crayons can be found in art stores or ordered online.

Create a work of art that conducts enough electricity to light an LED.

Fig. 5: Does the bulb get brighter as you move it closer to the clip?

MATERIALS
→ Printer paper
→ 1 graphite pencil or crayon (softer is better; we used a #9B graphite crayon)
→ 2 alligator clip test leads
→ Several small LEDs
→ 1 (9 volt) battery

PROTOCOL
1. Gather your supplies (fig. 1).

2. On a piece of printer paper, draw a thick, black rectangle about ½ inch (1 cm) wide and 1½ inches (4 cm) long using a graphite pencil or crayon. Color over it again and again until you create a solid layer of graphite. This lab won't work if there are any spaces or gaps (fig. 2).

3. Connect one end of each alligator clip to one of a battery terminal.

4. Clip the other end of the alligator clip attached to the positive (+) battery terminal to the long leg of an LED bulb.

5. Touch the free wire of the LED bulb to the right side of the graphite bar you drew (fig. 3).

6. Touch the alligator clip attached to the negative (−) battery terminal to the left side of the graphite bar you drew (fig. 4).

7. Move the LED wire closer to the alligator clip to see what happens. The light should get brighter as you decrease the distance. Try not to touch the bulb directly to the clip (fig. 5).

Fig. 1: Gather your supplies.

Fig. 2: Draw and trace with graphite.

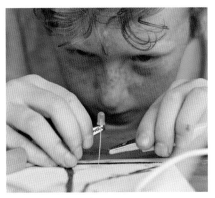

Fig. 3: Touch the free LED bulb wire to the graphite bar.

Fig. 4: Touch the metal alligator clip to the graphite bar on the other side.

8. If the bulb doesn't light up, switch the positive alligator clip to the other leg of the LED bulb and try it again. If it still doesn't work, make sure there are no gaps in the line you drew and then try a different LED.

9. Make some new drawings with the graphite pencil or crayon. Can the electrical current travel around corners or curves? What happens if you erase part of the drawing to create a gap?

CREATIVE ENRICHMENT

→ Use graphite to create a light-up comic strip or comic book with characters or features you can use as circuits to light LEDs.

THE
STEAM
BEHIND THE FUN:

Graphite is a crystalline form of carbon. Artists use it for drawing because it can be used to form everything from sharp lines to gorgeous smudges can be easily erased.

Often used to make pencil lead, graphite is a special material called a *conductor*. Conductors are substances that electrical current can flow through. Some metals are conductors as well.

Because graphite is a conductor, it can be used to create a circuit—a path for electrical current. Here, the solid graphite line you draw on paper—that thin layer of graphite you lay down—carries enough electrical charge to light a bulb.

ART BOT

`0 1 1 1 0 1 0 1 1 1 1 0 1 0 1 0 1 0 1 0 1 0 0 0 1 0 1 1 1 1 0 1 0 1 0 0 0 0 0 0 1 0 0 0 0 0 0 0 1 0 1 0 1 1 1 1`

SAFETY TIPS AND HINTS

→ Adult supervision is required when using a utility knife.

→ Test your motor by attaching the battery clip or the alligator clips to the battery holder terminals. If it's working, the cork should spin. If not, try switching the alligator clips to the opposite terminals.

In this lab, you build a simple robot that can draw.

Fig. 5: Tape markers to the outside of the cup and attach the clip to the battery to start.

MATERIALS

→ 1 cork
→ 1 (3 volt) toy or hobby DC (direct current) motor
→ 1 (18 fluid ounce, or 535 ml) plastic cup
→ Scissors or utility knife
→ 2 alligator clip test leads
→ Duct tape
→ AA battery holder
→ 2 AA batteries
→ Battery clip (optional)
→ Dry erase board markers or washable markers
→ Dry erase board or paper

→ Decorating objects such as markers, plastic eyes, pom-poms, and pipe cleaners

PROTOCOL

1. Attach a cork to the moving part of the toy motor.

2. Cut a hole in the bottom of the cup large enough for the motor terminals to poke through, but smaller than the motor itself. Be sure the moving part of the motor points straight up.

3. Attach the alligator clips to the motor by clipping them onto wires or directly onto the motor terminals (**fig. 1**).

4. Tape the connections and tape the motor to the top of the cup so the cork can still spin (**fig. 2**).

5. Secure an AA battery holder to the inside of the cup using duct tape and insert the batteries (**fig. 3**).

6. Attach a battery clip (if using) to the free ends of the alligator clips (**fig. 4**). Tape the wires inside the cup.

Fig. 1: Attach the motor to alligator clips through a hole in the top of a plastic cup.

Fig. 2: Tape the connections and the motor to the cup so it can still spin.

Fig. 3: Tape an AA battery holder to the inside of the cup and insert the batteries.

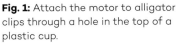

Fig. 4: Secure alligator clips and attach a battery clip (optional).

7. Tape 3 or 4 markers to the outside of your cup, marker-side down. Space them evenly and try to attach them so they extend an equal distance from the bottom of the cup. Connect the motor to the battery holder using the clips or the battery snap **(fig. 5)**.

8. Remove the lids from the markers and set your art bot on a piece of paper or a dry erase board.

9. Watch your art bot go. Does it create dots or lines?

CREATIVE ENRICHMENT

→ Experiment with moving the cork to see how that changes the balance and affects your bot's ability to draw. How does moving the markers to different heights on the side of the cup affect balance and drawing ability?

THE
STEAM
BEHIND THE FUN:

The cork attached to the motor adds unbalanced weight to the spinning part of the motor and the resulting vibrations cause the art bot to scoot around on its marker "legs," creating random patterns on the paper or dry board below.

Since the 1970s, artists have been programming computers to paint and draw, using guidelines called *algorithms*. Today, computers are able to find images in clouds, create color palettes, paint in different styles, or even choose idea-based themes for their work. But even as computers learn, adapt, and become more proficient at creating images, whether the work they create is really original art remains a question, as it will always reflect the ideas of the artist who first programmed them.

DESKTOP BEAD BUBBLER

011101011110101010101010100010111101010000001000000010101111

SAFETY TIPS AND HINTS

→ Plastic beads are a choking hazard; young children should have adult supervision when doing this project.

→ Poke holes near the top of the bottle before turning the pump on, so air can escape easily.

→ Wear safety glasses when making a hole in the bottle cap.

Use an aquarium pump to design a piece of moving art.

Fig. 5: Watch the beads move.

MATERIALS

→ Protective glasses
→ Hammer
→ Nail
→ Clear 2 quart (2 L) bottle with cap
→ Screwdriver (optional)
→ 2 to 3 feet (30 to 60 cm) flexible tubing to fit the pump
→ Rubber band
→ Rock or weight small enough to fit through the mouth of the 2 quart (2 L) bottle
→ Small air pump, such as an aquarium pump
→ Water
→ Beads
→ Oil, such as vegetable oil

PROTOCOL

1. Use a hammer and nail to make a hole in the center of the bottle cap **(fig. 1)**.

2. If needed, use a screwdriver to make the hole large enough for the tubing.

3. Push the tubing through the hole in the lid.

4. With a rubber band, attach a small rock or weight to one end of the tubing.

5. Attach the other end of the tubing to the pump.

6. Push the weighted end (with the rock) of the tubing into the bottle so the rock or weight is suspend just above the bottom.

7. Fill the bottle halfway with water.

8. Add beads to the bottle.

9. Use the oil to fill the bottle almost to the top, leaving 3 to 4 inches (7.5 to 10 cm) below the threads for the cap **(fig. 2)**. Screw the lid on.

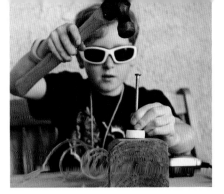

Fig. 1: Use a nail to make a hole in the bottle cap.

Fig. 2: Add water, beads, and oil to the bottle.

Fig. 3: Plug in the pump.

Fig. 4: See what happens.

10. Poke several holes in the air space at the top of the bottle, near the cap, so air can escape.

11. Plug the air pump in to start creating bubbles **(fig. 3)**.

12. Guess what will happen to the oil, water, and beads when you add air bubbles to the mix **(figs. 4 and 5)**.

CREATIVE ENRICHMENT

→ Try this experiment using different materials or different ratios of oil to water. What materials could you use to create lifelike fish that would move around in a bubbler like this one?

THE
STEAM
BEHIND THE FUN:

An emulsion is a mixture of two things that normally can't be mixed together easily—and oil and water are two such liquids. Water molecules would much rather stick to each other than to oil molecules. The feeling is mutual, and oil molecules aren't attracted to water either.

Liquid water has tightly packed molecules and is denser than oil, so it sinks to the bottom of the bottle. Air is less dense than both water and oil, so, when you turn on the air pump, bubbles emerge from the tubing and move to the top of the bottle. As a result, the oil and water start to move, mixing with bubbles and beads, creating a large-scale, emulsion-like mixture of oil, water, beads, and air.

SEWABLE CIRCUITS

`0 1 1 1 0 1 0 1 1 1 1 0 1 0 1 0 1 0 1 0 1 0 1 0 0 0 1 0 1 1 1 1 0 1 0 1 0 0 0 0 0 0 1 0 0 0 0 0 0 0 1 0 1 0 1 1 1 1`

SAFETY TIPS AND HINTS

→ Young children should have adult supervision using sewing needles and coin cell batteries.

→ To make this project simple, use a battery holder with a switch and a single LED. See steps 10 and 11 in this lab for instructions.

→ Be sure the thread connecting the positive (+) holes doesn't touch or cross the thread connecting the negative (−) holes or your light won't work.

Whip up some lighted textiles using conductive thread to complete a circuit.

Fig. 4: Your sewable circuit is complete!

MATERIALS

→ Ruler
→ Scissors
→ Sewing needle
→ Sewing thread
→ Sewable coin cell battery holder with an ON/OFF switch or a sewable coin cell battery holder
→ Coin cell battery that fits into the battery holder
→ 1 or more sewable LEDs

→ 1 or more pieces of heavy fabric, such as felt
→ Uncoated sewable metal snaps (optional)
→ 1 or 2 small pieces of fabric (optional)
→ Conductive thread
→ Embroidery hoop (optional)
→ Glue

PROTOCOL

1. Design your project. Decide where you want to place the battery holder and the LEDs. Be sure to leave enough room between them for several stiches. Remember, if you will be using snaps to connect the circuit, you can cover the battery holder with fabric as you finish up, but if the battery holder has a switch, you will need to be able to access it.

2. Use a sewing needle and sewing thread (nonconductive) to anchor a battery holder and sewable LED(s) onto the fabric—just make one or two loops through each hole (fig. 1).

Fig. 1: Anchor the battery holder and LED(s) onto the fabric.

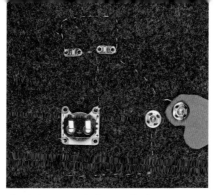

Fig. 2: Sew LED lights to the battery, to each other, and to a snap.

Fig. 3: Closing the snap will complete the circuit.

3. If you're using snaps, with sewing thread and a sewing needle, tack half a metal snap onto a separate small piece of fabric.

4. Cut a 12 inch (30 cm) piece of conductive thread and thread it through a sewing needle. Knot one end and pull it up through the positive (+) hole in the battery holder. Push it back down just outside the negative (+) hole. Repeat several times to form a tight connection between the holder and the thread. Be sure there is plenty of conductive thread contacting the metal. Do not cut the thread.

5. Using the same thread, make a running stitch **(fig. 2)** to sew a path to the positive (+) hole in the LED and sew around the negative (+) hole in the LED several times, as you did with the battery. Now, sew a running stitch to connect the positive (+) hole of a second LED, if you have one. Knot the thread and cut off the excess.

6. With a second 12 inch (30 cm) piece of conductive thread and using a running stitch that avoids touching any components, connect the negative (−) holes of the two LEDs. Continue a running stitch to one side and use the same thread to reinforce the snap on the small piece of fabric, sewing around the entire snap to form a good connection.

7. Cut a third 12 inch (30 cm) piece of conductive thread and use it to tack down the negative (−) hole of the battery holder. Use a running stich to sew down one half of a snap a few inches (7.5 cm) from the battery board. Knot it and cut the thread **(fig. 2)**.

8. To light the LED, close the snap **(figs. 3 and 4)**.

THE STEAM
BEHIND THE FUN:

Conductive thread is made from nylon coated with silver or another conductive material. It's flexible enough to sew with and can carry enough electrical current to light LEDs.

When you use the thread to connect the positive (+) and negative (−) terminals of a battery to a light bulb, you complete an electrical circuit, which lights the bulb.

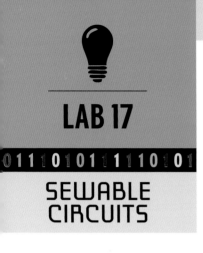

Fig. 6: Glue on decorations to embellish your electric art.

Fig. 5: You can cover the battery holder with fabric.

9. Complete your design. You can cover the battery holder and attach decorations using sewing (nonconductive) thread or glue. **(figs. 5 and 6)**.

10. If you are using a battery holder with a switch and a single LED: Thread a 12 inch (30 cm) piece of conductive thread through a sewing needle. Knot one end and pull it up through the positive (+) hole in the battery holder. Push it back down just outside the positive (+) hole and repeat several times to form a tight connection. Be sure there is plenty of conductive thread contacting the metal.

11. Using the same thread, create a running stitch to sew a path from the positive (+) hole in the battery holder to the positive (+) hole in the LED and sew around the positive (+) hole in the LED several times, as you did with the battery. Knot the thread and cut off the excess.

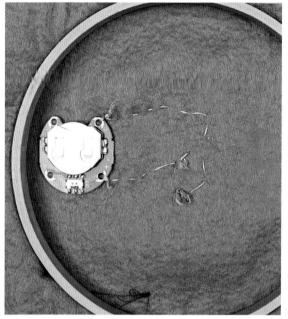

Fig. 7: You can also sew a light to a battery with a switch.

Fig. 8: Ta da!

12. Repeat the process with a second 12 inch (30 cm) piece of conductive thread, anchoring it to the negative (−) hole in the battery holder, making a running stitch to the negative (−) hole in the LED, sewing around the negative (−) hole, and knotting the thread as before. Turn the switch to ON to light the LED **(figs. 7 and 8)**.

CREATIVE ENRICHMENT

→ Once you've got the hang of it, try connecting more lights to your design.
→ Fashion and home designers sometimes incorporate sewable LEDs into textiles. Create your own functional or fashionable design for a piece of clothing or furniture that utilizes this technology.

WIND TURBINE

Generate enough power to light an LED using your breath or a blow dryer.

Fig. 5: Try using a blow dryer!

SAFETY TIPS AND HINTS

→ Adult supervision is required for this lab. Keep blow driers away from water.

→ Use a pinwheel fan if you don't want to make your own.

MATERIALS

→ Pencil
→ Drawing compass
→ Ruler
→ Cardboard
→ Scissors
→ Glue gun and glue sticks
→ Craft sticks
→ Alligator clip test leads
→ 1 micromotor for wind turbine generator or 3 phase AC generator model (see resources)
→ LED
→ Blowdryer (optional)

PROTOCOL

1. Use a compass and ruler to draw a circle that is 4¾ inches (12 cm) in diameter (from one side to the other) on your cardboard.

2. Place the point of your compass on the line of the circle and draw another circle the same size.

3. Align your ruler with the two holes made by the compass and draw a line that bisects both circles. Draw a third circle with its center at the point the ruler crossed the original circle.

4. Use your ruler to draw a line perpendicular to the first line you drew. Then, draw two more circles with their center where that line intersects the original circle.

5. Use the points where the circles intersect to draw two more lines, dividing the circle into 8 even segments **(fig. 1)**.

6. Draw a 1½ inch (4 cm) circle inside the center circle, using the same center point.

Fig. 1: Use a compass and ruler to create a cardboard circles divided into 8 sections.

Fig. 2: Glue craft sticks to reinforce.

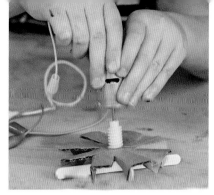

Fig. 3: Attach alligator clips to the motor and glue the motor to the fan.

7. Use scissors to cut out the original 4¾ inch (12 cm) circle.

8. Cut notches along the 8 lines you made, from the outside of the circle to the inner circle. Bend the blades up, all in the same direction.

9. Hot glue craft sticks to the fan blades to reinforce them (**fig. 2**).

10. Attach alligator clips to each terminal of the motor. Firmly attach the motor to the fan using hot glue and the glue gun (**fig. 3**).

11. Attach an LED to the other ends of the alligator clips.

Fig. 4: Blow hard on the fan blade to spin it and light up the LED.

12. Blow on the fan as hard as you can or use a blow dryer to spin it. Watch for the LED to light up. If it doesn't, switch the alligator clips on the LED (**figs. 4 and 5**).

THE STEAM BEHIND THE FUN:

Harnessing the wind's power is a clean way to generate electricity.

Many wind turbines only have three blades, but they work in a similar manner to the one you created in this project. Moving air turns the blades, which are attached to a rotor. The rotor is attached to a piece of metal called a *shaft*, which turns inside a generator, creating electricity by moving charged particles, called *electrons*, from one place to another.

CREATIVE ENRICHMENT

→ Build different kinds of turbine blades to connect to a motor. Test them to see which ones work best.

LAB 19

CD BOT

`0 1 1 0 1 0 1 1 1 1 0 1 0 0 1 0 1 0 1 0 1 0 1 0 0 0 1 0 1 1 1 1 1 0 1 0 0 0 0 0 1 0 0 0 0 0 0 0 1 0 1 0 1 1 1 1 1`

Create moving, spinning robots from old CDs and toothbrushes.

Fig. 5: Clip the motor to the battery holder and let your robot go!

MATERIALS

→ AA battery holder
→ 1 compact disc (CD)
→ Glue (a glue gun and glue sticks are best)
→ 2 AA batteries
→ 4 bottle caps
→ Alligator clip test leads or battery snap
→ 1 small (3 volt) toy motor
→ Duct tape or electrical tape
→ 4 similar toothbrushes
→ Cork
→ Decorations such as tape, pipe cleaners, sequins, or paint (optional)

PROTOCOL

1. Center an AA battery holder on a CD and firmly glue or tape it down. Insert the batteries.

2. Space 4 bottle caps evenly around the battery holder and glue them down (**fig. 1**).

3. Attach alligator clips or a battery snap or to the motor's terminals or wires (**fig. 2**). Tape the connections.

4. Glue 4 toothbrushes, brush-side away from the CD, onto the bottle caps, with the brushes on the outside (**fig. 3**).

5. Attach a cork to the motor and glue or tape the motor to the top of the CD so the cork can spin freely (**fig. 4**).

Fig. 1 Firmly glue or tape an AA battery holder and bottle caps to one side of a CD.

Fig. 2: Attach alligator clips or a battery snap to the motor.

Fig. 3: Glue 4 toothbrushes, brush side away from the CD, onto the bottle caps.

Fig. 4: Attach a cork to the motor and attach it to the top of the CD so it can spin.

6. Decorate your robot!

7. Clip the motor to the battery holder using the alligator clips or the battery snap.

8. Set the robot down and let it go **(fig. 5)**!

CREATIVE ENRICHMENT

→ Design another robot that uses bristles to move. Test how the type or arrangement of the brushes affects the movement.

THE
STEAM
BEHIND THE FUN:

Bristle bots move as the result of the vibrations transferred from an unbalanced motor through some rigid materials and into a large number of bristles. They are very simple robots, and the direction of their initial movement is largely dependent on the overall angle of their bristles.

You may observe that when a bristle bot bumps into an obstacle, it keeps moving. During the collision, there is an equal and opposite force between the object and the bot, which changes the direction of motion.

Some animals use bristles for locomotion. Polychaete worms, or bristle worms, have tiny leglike appendages with hairlike bristles sticking out. These bristles can have a number of functions, but they are often used for movement.

GADGET-READY GLOVES

SAFETY TIPS AND HINTS

→ Young children should have adult supervision using sewing needles.

Make any pair of gloves gadget-ready using conductive thread.

Fig. 5: The thread conducts current from your finger to the device.

MATERIALS

→ **Sewing needle**
→ **Conductive thread**
→ **Knit gloves**
→ **Cork** (optional)

PROTOCOL

1. Thread a sewing needle with 12 inches (30 cm) of conductive thread **(fig. 1)**. Knot one end of the thread.

Fig. 1: Thread a sewing needle with conductive thread.

Fig. 2: Sew small stitches into the index fingertip of the glove (use a cork to support your stitching).

Fig. 3: Tie off the thread.

Fig. 4: Try it out!

2. Place a cork or other object into the index finger of the glove (right or left glove, depending on whether you're right-handed or left-handed) to support your stitching. Sew 10 to 20 small overlapping stiches into the fingertip of the glove **(fig. 2)**.

3. Tie off the thread and cut off the excess **(fig. 3)**.

4. Put the glove on and test it on a touch screen device **(figs. 4 and 5)**.

5. If it doesn't work, add more stitches and test it again.

CREATIVE ENRICHMENT

→ Can you think of another good use for conductive thread? Try making sewable circuits (see Lab 17, page 50).

THE
STEAM
BEHIND THE FUN:

Our bodies are powered by chemical reactions that produce energy. Electrical activity from chemical reactions powers our heartbeats and regulates the rhythm—even our skin can conduct an electrical charge.

The touch screens on many electronic devices are designed to sense your skin's electricity and respond to a human touch, but they need a direct connection to the electrons (electricity-producing particles) in your skin.

When you put gloves on, the electrons can't move from your finger to the touch screen. However, if your finger is touching conductive thread, the electrons on your finger use the metal on the thread as a path to the device. This allows you to use your device while wearing gloves.

Touché! In the sport of fencing, conductive thread technology is used to detect when a fencing foil (sword) touches the conductive thread in a jacket worn by a competitor.

UNIT 03

ENGINEERING

THE WORD *ENGINEERING* IS DERIVED FROM THE LATIN WORD *INGENIARE*, WHICH REFERS TO INVENTION AND DESIGN. THE EARLIEST USE OF THE WORD *ENGINEER* COMES FROM THE ANCIENT ROMANS AND WAS USED TO DESCRIBE PEOPLE WHO MADE MACHINES OF WAR. TODAY, ENGINEERING ENCOMPASSES A FIELD THAT'S ENORMOUSLY DIVERSE IN SCOPE.

Civil engineers design cities, roads, and waterways. In ancient times, they designed aqueducts to carry clean water from one place to another and impossibly large and beautiful pyramids to memorialize pharaohs.

With the Industrial Age came coal and electricity, creating more jobs for engineers as the world sprang to life mechanically. Today, they make solar panels, design cars, create efficient heating and cooling systems for buildings, design medical devices, improve communication, and invent countless other ways to make our lives more safe and comfortable.

This unit gives you a starting point for some things you can design and build with your own hands. More importantly, it encourages you to set your mind in motion and improve the designs to make them work better, faster, or just to make them more fun.

"In science, you form hypotheses, do research, and test those against what you think happens before you proceed to design a product. In filmmaking, my process is fairly similar—I often have a loose idea of what the story is and from there I do research and see how that matches up before formulating how to go about telling that story. As an engineer, I learned to ask questions, be curious, and always look for the why—that is something that I've carried with me to filmmaking and it's made all the difference in how I approach storytelling."
—*Joyce Tsang, Emmy-winning filmmaker, mechanical engineer, and US patent holder*

RUBBER BAND SHOOTER

`0111010111101010101010100010111101010000000100000000010101111`

SAFETY TIPS AND HINTS

→ Adult supervision is required when using a glue gun.

→ Rubber band shooters should not be pointed at people.

Engineer a rubber band shooter for maximum distance and accuracy.

Fig. 4: Stretch a rubber band between the notches and the clothespin.

MATERIALS
→ Glue gun and glue sticks
→ Clothespin
→ Wooden paint stick or ruler
→ Needlenose pliers
→ Paint (optional)
→ Rubber bands

PROTOCOL

1. Glue a clothespin to one end of a paint stick or ruler so it opens toward the opposite end **(fig. 1)**.

2. Use needlenose pliers to make 2 parallel notches in the end of the wooden stick opposite the clothespin **(fig. 2)**.

3. Decorate the rubber band shooter with paint, if you'd like. Search the internet for some Australian Aboriginal boomerang decorations for inspiration or create your own design **(fig. 3)**.

4. Stretch a rubber band between the clothespin and the notches **(fig. 4)**.

5. Point the notched end at a target, not another person! Open the clothespin to shoot the rubber band.

6. Can you hit the target? Does your accuracy depend on the size of the rubber band you use **(fig. 5)**?

Fig. 1: Glue a clothespin to a paint stick or ruler.

Fig. 2: Use needlenose pliers to make 2 notches in the end of the stick opposite the clothespin.

Fig. 3: Decorate the rubber band shooter.

Fig. 5: Can you hit a target?

CREATIVE ENRICHMENT

→ Create rubber band shooters with variable distances between the notches and clothespin and test your designs to determine which is optimal for distance and accuracy.

→ Make your own paint (see Lab 32, page 92) and use it to decorate your rubber band shooter.

THE
STEAM
BEHIND THE FUN:

Stretching a rubber band stores energy in the form of elastic energy. How much energy is stored depends on how much rubber is stretched and how far it is stretched. When you release one end of the rubber band, by opening the clothespin, the rubber contracts and the elastic energy is transformed into kinetic energy, which is the energy of motion. The rubber band flies forward, off the stick and into the air.

Air resistance slows the rubber band and gravity pulls it toward earth, so you may have to aim your rubber band shooter a bit above the target to hit its center.

Humans have been decorating weapons for thousands of years. From spear handles and boomerangs to swords and shields, some weapons are works of art—featuring intricate designs, sacred symbols, and family crests.

POP-UP BOOKS

SAFETY TIPS AND HINTS

→ If card stock isn't working well for a particular fold or design, try using a lighter-weight paper, like printer paper.

Engineer your own pop-up designs using paper and scissors.

Fig. 6: Use your designs to make a pop-up book.

MATERIALS

→ **Card stock or small greeting cards**
→ **Scissors**
→ **Glue**
→ **Notebook**
→ **Markers**
→ **Colored paper**

PROTOCOL

1. Begin by making a V-fold. Fold a piece of paper in half or use a folded card.

2. Cut a diagonal line on a folded card and crease it down from both sides **(fig. 1)**.

3. Open and close the card to watch it pop out **(fig. 2)**.

4. Glue it into your notebook so the shape pops out when you open the book.

5. Create a layer by making 2 identical parallel cuts in a piece of folded paper **(fig. 3)**.

6. Test how it pops out.

7. Glue it into your book and attach a shape you'd like to have pop out **(fig. 4)**. Use markers and colorful paper to add details to your pop-up design.

8. Create more pop-out designs **(fig. 5)**.

9. Save your designs by gluing them into a book, creating a pop-up book **(fig. 6)**.

Fig. 1: Cut a diagonal line on a folded card and crease it down from both sides.

Fig. 2: Watch the shape pop out as you open and close the card.

Fig. 3: Make 2 parallel cuts to pop out a layer.

Fig. 4: The sun pops out!

Fig. 5: What other shapes can you create?

CREATIVE ENRICHMENT

→ Design pull-tabs that make things in your book move. Research more types of folds used in pop-up art and try them.

→ Write and illustrate a story using a pop-up book. Design the book before you start cutting, but let inspiration be your guide—and don't be afraid to change your ideas as you go.

THE STEAM BEHIND THE FUN:

Pop-up books are a great hands-on way to explore engineering by turning a two-dimensional piece of paper into a three-dimensional moving creation. While V-folds make things move in an arc, layers are boxes that open up and are used for structure.

Engineers often design objects and test them virtually on computers, but pop-ups demonstrate that building things yourself is sometimes the quickest, easiest way to learn how they work. In fact, experts say there's no substitute for handbuilding when it comes to pop-up designs.

Best of all, paper is inexpensive to play with and you can get it in many different thicknesses. You can decorate it easily using color and design, so your imagination is the only limit to what you can create.

LAB 23

BALLOON ROCKET

SAFETY TIPS AND HINTS

→ Adult supervision is required when children climb on chairs or trees to tie strings.

Create a rocket on string using a balloon and a straw.

Fig. 6: Try it from the other direction. What did you observe?

MATERIALS
→ String
→ Chair
→ Scissors
→ 3 plastic drinking straws
→ Balloon
→ Clothespin or bag clamp
→ Tape

PROTOCOL
1. Tie one end of a string to a tree branch or other object 3 feet (1 m) or more off the ground (fig. 1).

2. Place a chair several yards (several meters) away from the spot where you've tied the string. Pull the string to the chair, which will serve as a launch pad. Cut the string, leaving a little extra.

3. If your straws are the bendable kind, use scissors to cut off the bumpy, bendable parts to create smooth straws (**fig. 2**).

4. Thread the string through 1 to 3 straws and tie it to the chair, at a point lower than the other end of the string (**fig. 3**).

5. Pull the chair away from the high point until the string is taut between the two points.

6. Blow up a balloon and clamp the end closed.

7. Tape the balloon to the straw closest to the high point, so the mouth of the balloon faces the chair (**fig. 4**).

Fig. 1: Tie one end of a string to a tree branch or other object 3 feet (1 m) off the ground.

Fig. 2: Cut drinking straws so they are smooth.

Fig. 3: Thread the string through the straws and tie it to the chair.

Fig. 4: Blow up a balloon, clamp the end closed, and tape it to the straw closest to the high point.

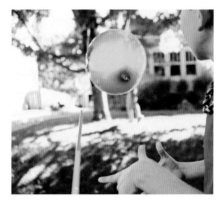

Fig. 5: Remove the clamp and send the balloon up the string.

8. When you're ready to launch, open the clip and let the balloon shoot up the string to the high point **(fig. 5)**.

9. Try it from the other direction. Which is faster **(fig. 6)**?

CREATIVE ENRICHMENT

→ Inflate balloons to different diameters and time how long it takes them to shoot to the high point to test whether air pressure changes speed.
→ Test what happens when you connect 2 inflated balloons to the same straw and shoot them up the string at the same time.

THE
STEAM
BEHIND THE FUN:

Newton's laws of motion tell us that for every action, there is an equal and opposite reaction.

Inflated balloons contain air under pressure from the stretched rubber of the balloon. When the mouth of the balloon is opened, the air leaving the balloon is pushed out by air pressure inside the balloon and an equal and opposite force launches the balloon rocket in the opposite direction.

Eventually, air resistance and gravity slow the balloon rocket and it stops moving.

RUBBER BAND RACER

SAFETY TIPS AND HINTS

→ Adult supervision is required when using a glue gun.

Make a race car from simple materials and measure how far it can go.

Fig. 8: On your mark, get set, go!

Fig. 1: Wrap cardboard around a spice bottle to make a tube.

Fig. 2: Find the center of each wheel using a square with intersecting diagonal lines.

Fig. 3: On either end of the tube, create two sets of holes that will hold two pencils parallel.

MATERIALS

→ Heavy cardboard
→ Spice bottle
→ Scissors
→ Duct tape or masking tape
→ 1 CD or a compass
→ Pencils
→ Ruler
→ Glue (a glue gun and glue sticks work best)
→ Wooden skewers
→ Plastic straw
→ Decorations
→ Thin rubber bands
→ Pipe cleaner (optional)

PROTOCOL

1. Wrap cardboard around a large spice bottle so you can see how it bends. Cut a piece of cardboard about 9 inches (23 cm) long to wrap around the bottle. Trim off the excess cardboard and tape it together to create a tube **(fig. 1)**.

2. Trace a CD, or use a compass, to make 8 circles on cardboard that are about 4½ inches (11.5 cm) in diameter. Use a ruler to make a square around each circle and then diagonal lines to mark the center of each circle. Cut out the circles. Glue 2 circles together, with the lines visible on the outside, until you have 4 wheels. Use skewers to poke holes through the center of each wheel **(fig. 2)**.

3. Poke 1 skewer through each end of the cardboard tube, about 1½ inches (4 cm) from the ends of the tube. Make sure the skewers are parallel and that they line up when you look through the end of the tube.

4. Use pencils to make the holes larger **(fig. 3)**.

5. Cut 4 (½ inch, or 1.5 cm) pieces off a straw. Glue them to the outside of each hole in the tube. Use a skewer to help align them. The skewer should spin freely **(fig. 4)**.

THE STEAM BEHIND THE FUN:

When you wind up the car, you use your body's energy to stretch the rubber band around the wooden skewer axle of a cardboard car. Energy is stored as elastic energy in the tightly stretched rubber bands. When you let go of the car, the rubber bands start to unwind. They apply enough force on the skewer to turn the wheels of the car, and the energy is transformed into the energy of motion, called *kinetic energy*.

011101011110101

RUBBER BAND RACER

Fig. 5: Decorate your car.

6. One at a time, put wheels on the skewers and glue the OUTSIDE of the wheel to the skewer. Make sure the wheels are parallel to the car, and to each other, as they dry. Cut off any excess skewer.

7. Decorate the car **(fig. 5)**!

8 Poke a skewer down the center of one end of the tube, parallel to the wheels, so it's sticking out about 1 inch (2.5 cm) **(fig. 6)**.

9. Tie 3 thin rubber bands together and hook them over the skewer that's sticking out. If you have a pipe cleaner or wire, hook it onto the other end of the rubber bands. Drop the rubber bands down through the center of the tube.

Fig. 4: Glue straws to the outside of each hole and add wheels.

Fig. 6: Add a skewer on one end to hold a rubber band.

Fig. 7: Wind the rubber bands until they are tight.

10. Grab the rubber bands from the end opposite where they are attached to the car. Remove the pipe cleaner hook and wind them around the skewer to create tension in the rubber bands. Wind them until they're tight **(fig. 7)**.

11. Set the car down and let the wheels start to spin to see which direction the car will go. When you're ready, let go **(fig. 8)**!

12. Measure how far the car traveled.

CREATIVE ENRICHMENT
→ Reengineer the car to go faster or farther. Try different kinds and numbers of rubber bands. How does changing wheel size affect speed and distance?

BRIDGE DESIGN

01110101011101010101010101010010101111101010010000010000000101011011

SAFETY TIPS AND HINTS

→ Adult supervision is required when using a glue gun.

Test your engineering and design skills by creating a bridge from pasta.

Fig. 4: Test your design.

MATERIALS

→ 2 shoeboxes or building blocks
→ Glue or glue gun and glue sticks
→ Pasta (spaghetti, linguine, or penne) or craft sticks

PROTOCOL

1. Set up 2 shoeboxes or blocks and decide how big a distance you want to span with your bridge (fig. 1).

2. Look up pictures on the internet of different types of bridges, such as beam bridges, arch bridges, cantilever bridges, suspension bridges, and truss bridges.

3. Design a simple bridge, such as a beam bridge, that has a horizontal structure and two supports—which are your boxes or blocks. Consider how the pasta will fit together and how you will reinforce it. How much weight do you want it to hold (fig. 2)?

4. Build the bridge by gluing together pieces of pasta or craft sticks (fig. 3). Let the glue dry.

5. When the bridge is dry, test it with boxes or cans of known weight to see how strong your design is. Record your results. Young kids can drive toy cars across their bridges (fig. 4).

6. Analyze your data and rebuild the bridge so it will hold more weight, if needed.

Fig. 1: Set up 2 objects to span.

Fig. 2: Design a bridge.

7. Consider the bridge's design. Can you make it more attractive without compromising its strength and durability?

8. Now, build a more complicated type of bridge.

Fig. 3: Use glue to build the strongest bridge you can make out of pasta.

CREATIVE ENRICHMENT

→ Research truss bridges and build different types of trusses from pasta. Which are the strongest? Which do you think are the most beautiful?
→ Look up some paintings and drawings of bridges on the internet. Create your own painting or model of a bridge in your neighborhood.

THE
STEAM
BEHIND THE FUN:

We wouldn't get far without bridges, and we depend on engineers to design strong and safe structures.

Two main forces act on a bridge. Gravity pushes down on the bridge, and the ground pushes up. The force from the ground acts on the structural materials in the bridge, which are subject to the forces of tension and compression.

If the tension or compression forces are too strong, a bridge can buckle, or even snap, which is why bridges are built using strong materials such as steel and concrete. Structures like trusses and cantilevers make bridges even stronger.

Arched bridges are very sturdy as well—some have been standing for more than two thousand years.

You'll discover bridges in everything from ancient Chinese art to impressionism to expressionism, serving as subject matter and background in many famous works.

GEAR CATERPILLAR

`0111010111101010101010100010111101010000001000000010101 11`

SAFETY TIPS AND HINTS

→ An adult should cut the cork and assist young children with hammering the nails through the cork circles.

→ Wear safety glasses when hammering the nail.

Make a gear train caterpillar using cardboard and cork gears.

Fig. 6: Paint and decorate your cork creation.

MATERIALS

→ Corrugated cardboard
→ Ruler
→ Pencil
→ Scissors
→ 2 or more corks
→ Serrated knife
→ Glue
→ Eye protection (safety glasses or sunglasses)
→ Small (about 1 inch, or 2 to 3 cm) nails
→ Hammer
→ Pie tin or disposable aluminum cake pan
→ Tape
→ Paint (optional)

PROTOCOL

1. Peel the paper off one side of some corrugated cardboard **(fig. 1)**.

2. Measure and cut the peeled cardboard into about ten (¾ inch, 2 cm, wide) strips **(fig. 2)**.

3. Have an adult cut a cork with a serrated knife into several ¾ inch (2 cm) thick circles.

4. Glue the cardboard strips, bumpy-side out, around the outside of each cork, trimming them as needed **(fig. 3)**.

5. Put on your safety glasses and pound a nail straight down through the center of each cork **(fig. 4)**.

6. Arrange the gears to create a caterpillar. Push the nails into the pie tin or cake pan so they interlock and spin together. Rearrange them as needed **(fig. 5)**,

Fig. 1: Peel the paper off one side of some corrugated cardboard.

Fig. 2: Measure and cut the peeled cardboard into thin strips.

Fig. 3: Glue the strips, bumpy-side-out, around the corks and trim them as needed.

Fig. 4: Pound a nail through the center of each cork.

Fig. 5: Arrange the gears and attach them to a pie tin or cake pan so they interlock and spin together.

7. Cover the nail points with more cork or tape to protect your hands from the sharp points.

8. Paint the gear caterpillar, if you like **(fig. 6)**. Give it a spin.

CREATIVE ENRICHMENT

→ Make another gear-powered animal or design. Use jar lids to make larger gears.

THE
STEAM
BEHIND THE FUN:

Some of the first gears we know about were created more than two thousand years ago by the Chinese and the Ancient Greeks. Gears are simple but extremely useful machines that transfer rotational force, or torque, from one gear to another. They're used in everything from mechanical clocks to mixers and oil rigs.

The bumps on gears are called *teeth*, or *cogs*.

If one gear meshes with a larger one, they turn at different speeds, creating a mechanical advantage at a lower speed or rotating the gears at a higher speed.

LAB 27

CAMERA OBSCURA

SAFETY TIPS AND HINTS

→ Adult supervision is required when using a utility knife and a glue gun.

Turn a shoebox into a simple camera that projects images.

Fig 8: Images are flipped by the lens.

Fig. 1: Cut one end off of a shoebox.

Fig. 2: Glue a magnifying glass into the remaining end of the box.

Fig. 3: Measure the height of the sides.

Fig. 4: Cut out 2 cardboard frames with windows to fit snugly inside the box.

MATERIALS

→ Shoebox
→ Scissors
→ Utility knife (optional)
→ Pencil
→ Magnifying glass
→ Glue gun and glue sticks
→ Cardboard
→ White tissue paper or other semitransparent paper
→ Craft sticks or skewers
→ Marker (optional)

PROTOCOL

1. Cut off one end of a shoebox (fig. 1).

2. Trace a magnifying glass lens on the other end of the shoebox and cut a hole for the glass.

3. Glue the magnifying glass into one end of the shoebox. You can break down the box to cut and glue and then re-tape it to make things easier **(fig. 2).**

THE STEAM BEHIND THE FUN:

When light travels through a very small hole, or a lens, an upside-down image is created. The flipped image results as light waves travel through the hole or lens and reemerge on the opposite side, with the reversed up/down orientation.

Leonardo da Vinci recorded some of the earliest descriptions and diagrams of these cameras in his notebooks, and in 1504, mathematician and astronomer Johannes Kepler coined the term "camera obscura." Kepler used a lens, rather than a pinhole, to project the sun's image. He also created a camera obscura that helped him draw landscapes.

A number of art historians believe some of the most famous seventeenth-century Dutch painters used camera obscuras to make their paintings more realistic and may have even projected images directly onto their canvases.

Fig. 6: Focus an image on the paper.

Fig. 5: Position white tissue paper between the two frames and glue the frames together.

4. Measure the height of the sides of the shoebox and the width of the inside of the box **(fig. 3)**.

5. Use your measurements to measure and cut out 2 cardboard squares approximately the same size as the end of the shoebox, but just a tiny bit smaller, so they can slide into the shoebox, parallel to the ends, without falling over.

6. Cut windows into the moveable cardboard pieces, leaving ½ inch (1 cm) of cardboard on each side **(fig. 4)**.

7. Glue a piece of white tissue paper to one of the cardboard windows so it's smooth and flat. Glue the other frame to the paper, sandwiching the paper between the two frames **(fig. 5)**.

8. Reinforce the cardboard windows along the edges using craft sticks or skewers.

9. Put the transparent window in the box, opposite the magnifying glass end.

Fig. 7: If your lens is too strong, build an extension.

10. Point the magnifying glass at an object outside and move the paper window back and forth in the box until you focus the image on the tissue paper **(fig. 6)**.

11. If the magnifying glass is very strong, you may have to build an extension on the box so you can move the paper window further away from the lens to focus **(fig. 7)**.

12. Notice that the image is flipped by the lens **(fig. 8)**.

CREATIVE ENRICHMENT
→ Trace the image you see on the tissue paper or make a larger camera obscura using a bigger box and a stronger lens. Try taping a piece of paper to a wall in a room with a window opposite the paper. Stand between the wall and window and use a magnifying glass to focus an image on the paper **(fig. 9)**.

Fig. 9: Trace the image on the tissue paper.

DISK DROP

01110101111010101010101010 0 0101 11110 101000000 1000 0000 101011 11

SAFETY TIPS AND HINTS

→ Adult supervision is required when using a glue gun.

→ Young children should have adult supervision around pushpins.

Design and build your own arcade game.

Fig. 6: Tape coins into the caps and play the game!

MATERIALS
→ Yardstick (meter stick)
→ Pencil
→ Large piece of cardboard or poster board (about 20 inches x 28 inches, or 51 x 71 cm) with side panels to help it stand (you can make these yourself)

→ Tennis ball can lid
→ Pushpins
→ 4 bottle caps
→ Glue gun and glue sticks
→ Large piece of clear plexiglass (plastic) that fits over most or all of the cardboard or poster board (plexiglass can be recycled from an old poster frame)
→ Craft sticks
→ Markers (optional)
→ Coins
→ Tape

PROTOCOL

1. Use a yardstick (meter stick) and a pencil to make vertical lines on the cardboard just wide enough for a tennis ball can cap to fall between **(fig. 1)**.

2. Place alternating rows of pushpins on the lines **(fig. 2)**.

3. Glue 1 bottle cap onto each corner of the poster board. These caps will hold the plexiglass **(fig. 3)**.

4. Cover the back of the pins with hot glue to coat the sharp points **(fig. 4)**.

Fig. 1: Draw vertical lines on the cardboard just wide enough for a tennis ball lid to fall between.

Fig. 2: Place alternating rows of pushpins on the lines.

Fig. 3: Glue bottle caps at each corner of the board to hold the plexiglass cover.

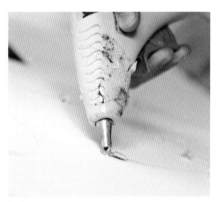

Fig. 4: Cover the backs of the pins with hot glue.

Fig. 5: Add the plastic cover, craft sticks, and scores to the game.

5. Glue the plexiglass onto the bottle caps to make a cover for the game.

6. Use glue to position craft sticks at the bottom of the game to guide the lid out of the game. Write scores in each slot **(fig. 5)**.

7. Tape coins into the tennis ball can cap to add weight and play the game **(fig. 6)**!

CREATIVE ENRICHMENT

→ Drop the lid down each slot at the top of your game 20 times and record where it comes out each time. Do you see a pattern?

→ Create another arcade game using household items. Can you make a pinball machine?

THE
STEAM
BEHIND THE FUN:

To design and build an arcade game, you have to engineer it so the pieces fit together correctly and the moving parts don't get stuck. In this case, gravity provides the force that moves the tennis ball can lid from the top of the game to bottom.

For seemingly random games like these, mathematicians use probability equations to predict which path a disk will take most often and where it will end up most frequently.

011101011110101010101010 010111110101000000100000000101011 1

SAFETY TIPS AND HINTS

→ Adult supervision is required when using a utility knife or glue gun.

→ This experiment is recommended for ages 10 and up and can be made using one or four strings. Using a single string will yield an instrument that's easier to pick out simple tunes on. The ukulele in this project is very simple and won't stay in tune well. However, it's a great way to practice design and problem solving skills.

Create a pluckable baritone ukulele using household items.

Fig. 5: Tie on and tune the strings.

MATERIALS

→ Duct tape
→ 3 wooden yardsticks (meter sticks)
→ 1 large (8 inch x 4 inch, or 20 x 10 cm) rectangular plastic container with a lid
→ Scissors
→ Utility knife (optional)
→ Craft sticks
→ Glue gun and glue sticks
→ Small metal screw eyes
→ 2 pencils
→ 1 nylon guitar or ukulele string or a set of 4 nylon ukulele strings
→ Eye protection (safety glasses or sunglasses)
→ Thin nail
→ Hammer

PROTOCOL

1. Gather together the yardsticks (meter sticks) in a stack, one on top of the other. Use duct tape to tape them together. Place tape on each end and at the 20 inch (50 cm) mark.

2. Cut a hole in the top third of one end of the plastic container lid, about 3 to 4 inches (7.5 to 10 cm) wide.

3. Use scissors or a utility knife to notch the lid and the ends of the plastic container so the taped yardsticks (meter sticks) can lie flat under the lid **(fig. 1)**.

4. Tape the lid to the container securely, with the yardstick (meter stick) under the lid and about 16 inches (40 cm) of yardstick

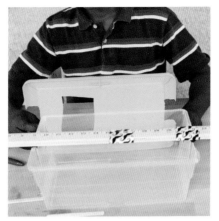

Fig. 1: Cut a hole in a lid and notch the ends so the taped yardsticks (meter sticks) lie flush with lid.

Fig. 2: Tape the lid and yardstick (meter stick) together securely.

(meter stick) extending on one end to create a neck for the ukulele **(fig. 2)**.

5. Cut a craft stick in half and glue down both pieces about 3½ inches (9 cm) from the end of the ukulele's neck. These sticks create a part of the instrument called the *nut*.

THE STEAM BEHIND THE FUN:

Sound is created by air molecules banging together to create vibrations, called *sound waves*. When you pluck a string, it vibrates, moving the air around it to create these waves. The sound travels through the hole you made, into the instrument where it is amplified. Ukuleles and guitars sound different depending on what the strings and the body are made from.

The speed of vibrations determines the pitch of the note created. Faster vibrations make higher-pitched sounds. When a string is tightened by turning tuning pegs (screw eyes in this case), it vibrates faster and sounds higher when you pluck it.

Fig. 4: Glue together 3 craft sticks. Glue them to the ukulele at the end farthest from the neck. Put a pencil behind them and glue another layer of craft sticks to secure the pencil.

Fig. 3: Add craft sticks (the nut) to the neck and put in the screw eyes.

6. Put on your safety glasses and use the thin nails to make guide holes for the screw eyes. Put from 1 to 4 screw eyes in the neck, depending on how many strings you want your ukulele to have **(fig. 3)**.

- **If using 1 string:** Center the screw eye about 1 inch (2.5 cm) above the nut.
- **If using 4 strings:** Position 2 screw eyes 1 inch (2.5 cm) above the nut and the other two screws eyes 1 inch (2.5 cm) above those, so they span the width of the neck, an equal distance apart—but with the 2 top screw eyes inside the 2 lower ones **(fig. 3)**.
- Screw them about halfway into the wood, leaving some space for the string(s) to wrap around.

7. Create a bridge by gluing together 3 craft sticks and then gluing them to the yardsticks (meter sticks) at the end farthest from the neck. Put a pencil behind them and glue another layer of craft sticks to secure the pencil **(fig. 4)**.

8. Position a second pencil on top of the craft sticks so strings can be threaded between the two pencils and tied onto the second pencil.

9. Depending on how many strings your ukulele has, tie the ukulele strings to each of the screw eyes in order (string 4 goes on the left side, and string 1 goes on the far right screw. The second thickest string will be second from the left, and wrap each string around its screw eye neck a few times. The order of notes will be tuned (from lowest to highest) to D G B E **(fig. 5)**.

10. Tie the strings to the pencil behind the bridge, pulling them tight before tying them on.

11. Make parallel notches in the craft sticks on each end of the ukulele to guide the strings, so they don't slide around.

12. Tighten the strings by turning the screw eyes to wind the strings around the screws. You may have to play around with this a bit.

13. Find an online baritone ukulele tuner or tune the 4 strings to D G B E (from a piano, pitch pipe, or other instrument you may have around the house) by turning the screw eyes. Tune your single string to D. Pick put a tune on the strings **(fig. 6)**.

Fig. 6: Can you play a tune?

CREATIVE ENRICHMENT

→ Figure out where to place frets on the neck so you can play chords. You may have to adjust the thickness of the craft sticks at the top of the neck.
→ Build a sturdier ukulele using a wooden box, a stronger thicker wooden neck, a metal nut, and a metal bridge to see whether it sounds better. You can make the nut and bridge using bolts.

SOLAR MARSHMALLOW COOKER

`01110101111010101010101010 0 0101111101010000000100000000101011111`

SAFETY TIPS AND HINTS

→ Be careful of sharp edges on mirrors.

→ For an extra treat, add chocolate and graham crackers and make s'mores.

Use the Sun's power to heat up delicious snacks.

Fig. 5: Put a marshmallow on a plate in the center of the box and close the lid.

MATERIALS

→ Shoebox or pizza box with hinged lid
→ Scissors
→ Tape
→ Plastic wrap
→ Aluminum foil
→ Glue
→ Small mirror(s) (optional)
→ Black paper
→ Styrofoam or newspaper
→ Colored markers
→ Marshmallows
→ Plate
→ Pencil or wooden skewer

PROTOCOL

1. Cut a flap in the shoebox or pizza box top, leaving 1 inch (2.5 cm) or so around each edge.

2. Tape plastic wrap over each side of the hinged window to create a double layer of plastic **(fig. 1)**.

3. Cover the inside of the flap with foil to create a solar reflector. Glue the foil on, if possible. If you have a mirror, or mirrors, attach them to the foil to provide extra reflection **(fig. 2)**. Place black paper on the floor of the box.

4. Put some foam or rolled-up newspaper around the inside edges of the box to act as insulation **(fig. 3)**.

5. Decorate your solar cooker **(fig. 4)**.

6. Take the box outside into direct sunlight. Put a marshmallow on a plate in the center of the box and close the lid **(fig. 5)**

Fig. 1: Cover the box window with a double layer of plastic wrap.

Fig. 2: Cover the inside of the flap with foil. Add black paper and mirrors.

Fig. 3: Add insulation.

Fig. 4: Decorate the box.

Fig. 6: Prop the flap open to focus sunlight on the marshmallow.

7. Use a pencil, skewer, or stick to prop the hinged reflector window open. Adjust the reflector to focus the sun's light on the marshmallow **(fig. 6)**.

8. Wait for the sun to heat the marshmallow.

9. When it's ready, enjoy your warm marshmallow snack.

CREATIVE ENRICHMENT

→ Design a bigger, more efficient solar oven. Use plexiglass rather than plastic wrap to make the window. What else could you try? Think about the angle of the reflective surfaces and how light hits the box.

THE
STEAM
BEHIND THE FUN:

The Sun's light carries lots of energy. Although the sun's light rays can easily travel though the plastic on your marshmallow oven, the heat energy carried by the rays is trapped inside the solar cooker.

While shiny foil and mirrors reflect sunlight into the box, dark paper helps to absorb the light, keeping the heat inside the box.

ART

UNIT 04

WHAT DO YOU THINK OF WHEN YOU HEAR THE WORD *ART*? A PAINTING? A STATUE? DOES ART REPRESENT THINGS IN EXACTLY THE WAY YOU'D EXPECT, OR SHOULD IT CHALLENGE THE WAY YOU SEE THE WORLD? IF YOU'RE NOT SURE, YOU'RE NOT ALONE.

Art is notoriously tough to define. It can be realistic or abstract. It can be created to convey beauty, like Katsushika Hokusai's gorgeous woodblock print of an ocean wave, or be woven into the fabric of a functional or religious object, like a carved African mask. Whether art is intentional or accidental, it is a window into our minds and cultures. It teaches us about the past, captures the present, and guesses at the future.

Sometimes, we recognize ourselves in art, and other times, it allows us to experience things we've never seen, heard, or even imagined. It helps us experience the world in new and surprising ways.

Running your hands over a bronze sculpture warmed by the sun is completely different than taking ten steps back to study it with your eyes alone. Turning the corner in a museum to discover that a painting you've only seen in a book takes up an entire wall is a wonderful shock. If you've ever been to a concert, you know that sound waves from live music can give you chills.

This unit plays with the visual arts and some of the tools, materials, and techniques that modern artists use to express themselves. The labs illustrate the fact that knowing a little science comes in handy when creating masterpieces.

"I started college as a graphic design major, and I still use those skills on a daily basis as a television producer. It's incredible how everything from composition to font selection to spatial relations can come in handy. I wouldn't trade that creative background for anything."
—*Christian Unser, senior producer,* Twin Cities Live

MARVELOUS MARBLED PAPER

`011101011110101010101010001011110101000000100000000101011111`

SAFETY TIPS AND HINTS

→ Allow two days for this project. On Day 1, prepare the paper and thickened water. On Day 2, marble the paper.

→ Adult supervision is required. Carrageenan works better than cornstarch for marbling, but don't be afraid to try it with cornstarch. It will still be lots of fun.

Create gorgeous marbled patterns by floating paint on thickened water and lifting the design onto alum-treated paper.

Fig. 8: Let the paper dry and show off your art.

Fig. 1: Make the carrageenan solution.

Fig. 2: Drip some paint onto the carrageenan solution in the pan.

MATERIALS

→ Large bowl
→ ⅜ cup (72 g) alum (aluminum sulfate), available online or at most grocery stores in the spice section
→ 1½ gallons (5.7 L) water, divided
→ Paintbrushes and/or eyedroppers
→ Sponge (optional)
→ Heavyweight craft paper or watercolor paper
→ Blender
→ 2 tablespoons (22 g) carrageenan (marbling size), divided (available online; alternatively, cornstarch may be substituted, see Note)
→ 1-gallon (3.8 L) container with a lid
→ Shallow trays or baking sheets
→ Liquid acrylic paint (several colors)
→ Toothpicks
→ Styrofoam strip (optional)

PROTOCOL

1. In a large bowl, mix together the alum and ½ gallon (1.9 L) of water. Brush or sponge the solution onto several pieces of heavy paper, like watercolor paper. Alternatively, dip the paper in the alum solution. Let the paper dry completely.

2. In a blender, blend 1 tablespoon (11 g) of carrageenan with ½ gallon (1.9 L) of water for 30 seconds. Pour into a large lidded container for storage.

3. In the blender, combine the remaining tablespoon (11 g) of carrageenan with the remaining ½ gallon (1.9 L) of water and mix again. Combine the two batches and let them sit overnight. The solution will keep for about 2 days (fig. 1).

THE STEAM BEHIND THE FUN:

To create lasting beautiful marbled designs, you have to float paint or ink on top of another liquid, create a design on it, and then get the colors to stick to a piece of paper or fabric.

Carrageenans are large, long chainlike molecules extracted from edible red seaweeds. Their size and flexibility give them a special ability to form gel-like substances. Carrageenans are often used to thicken dairy products, like yogurt, but in this lab, we use them to thicken water so paint will float on top of it.

Alum is a special chemical called a *mordant*. Mordants are good at combining with other chemicals so they get stuck and can't move around much. Alum is often used in dying textiles, like the cloth used to make your clothes, but other mordants can be used to stain other things, like bacterial cells. In this project, the alum on the paper acts as a mordant by combining with the paint and making it stick to the paper.

0111010111110101

MARVELOUS MARBLED PAPER

Fig. 3: Drip or spatter more paint onto the carrageenan.

NOTE: To make the solution with cornstarch instead of carrageenan: In a small bowl, dissolve ¼ cup (32 g) of cornstarch in ½ cup (120 ml) of cold water. In a saucepan over high heat, bring 6 cups (1.4 L) of water to a boil. Stir the cornstarch solution into the water. Stir well and boil for 1 minute. Turn the heat to low and simmer for 2 minutes more, stirring occasionally. Remove from the heat, cool, and thin to the consistency of heavy cream by adding water as needed.

4. Pour a thin layer of carrageenan (or cornstarch) solution into a shallow tray.

5. Add water to the acrylic paint and mix until it is the consistency of whole milk.

6. Drip or use a brush to spatter the thinned paint into the solution. Be creative and cover the entire surface with paint **(figs. 2 and 3)**.

7. Use toothpicks to make marbled patterns **(fig. 4)**.

Fig. 4: Use toothpicks to make marbled designs.

Fig. 5: Or use a tool to create more complex patterns.

Fig. 6: Place a piece of treated paper on the design.

8. You can place toothpicks in a strip of Styrofoam to make a uniform dragging tool to create more complicated repeated patterns **(fig. 5)**.

9. When your design is complete, carefully place a piece alum-treated paper on it and smooth it to remove any air underneath **(fig. 6)**.

10. Carefully remove the paper by lifting it out of the paint. You can drag it against the edge of the pan to remove excess paint, if you wish **(fig. 7)**.

11. Briefly rinse the colorful paper in the sink to remove extra paint and see the design more clearly.

12. Let your artwork dry and show it off **(fig. 8)**.

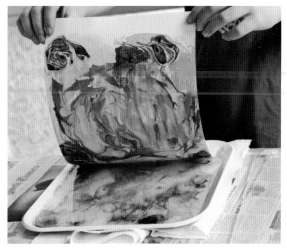

Fig. 7: Carefully lift the paper from the tray.

CREATIVE ENRICHMENT
→ Use the paper you created to make bookmarks, notebook covers, or in a pop-up book (Lab 22).

HOMEMADE PAINT

SAFETY TIPS AND HINTS

→ Check the warnings on dried pigments before you purchase them. Some are toxic and must be handled carefully. Avoid inhaling pigments.

Mix up some masterpiece-worthy homemade paint using clay and dried pigments.

Fig. 5: Create a masterpiece!

MATERIALS
→ Bowl
→ ½ cup (63 g) all-purpose flour, plus more as needed
→ Water
→ ¼ cup (36 g) EPK powdered clay, also called EPK kaolin (can be ordered online; we got ours at continentalclay.com)
→ Several small containers
→ Dried pigments, such as iron oxide, zinc oxide, black iron oxide, and ultramarine blue
→ Paintbrushes
→ Paper or fabric to paint on

PROTOCOL

1. In a medium bowl, stir together the flour and ½ cup (120 ml) of cold tap water. Mix well (fig. 1).

2. Add ¼ cup (60 ml) of hot tap water and mix well to combine.

3. Add the powdered clay and stir until smooth.

4. Continue adding flour and water until the paint has the consistency you want (fig. 2).

5. Separate the paint into several containers.

6. Add pigment to the paint and mix, adding more pigment until the desired color is achieved (figs. 3 and 4).

7. Use the paint to make designs on paper or fabric (fig. 5).

8. Leftover paint can be refrigerated in an airtight container for a week or so.

Fig. 1: Measure the flour, powdered clay, and water.

Fig. 2: Mix everything well.

Fig. 3: Add pigment to the paint and mix.

Fig. 4: Test out the colors.

CREATIVE ENRICHMENT

→ Make some other types of paint. Artists used to use egg as a binder in tempera paint. Look up a recipe online and use the pigments from this lab to make tempera.

THE STEAM BEHIND THE FUN:

We see colors as the result of light rays reflected back at our eyes by different compounds. For example, green grass absorbs every wavelength of light except those in the green spectrum, which are reflected back at our eyes.

Pigments are molecules that give things color, and the clay-based paint in this lab is colored with natural pigments.

One type of pigment, called *iron oxide*, is a combination of iron and oxygen and can range in color from yellow to red to black. While red zinc oxide reflects reddish light waves, black iron oxide absorbs all the colors in the visible spectrum. Zinc oxide is the opposite and reflects all the colors, appearing white.

Archeologists and scientists believe prehistoric artists used earth minerals, such as red iron oxide and black charcoal, to create cave paintings.

HANDMADE PAPER

Create beautiful, handmade paper by recycling scraps.

Fig. 5: When the paper is dry, carefully peel it off the screen.

MATERIALS
→ Paper shredder or scissors
→ Several sheets of scrap paper
→ Bowl
→ Water
→ Blender
→ Food coloring
→ Glitter (optional)
→ Cookie cutters or canning jar lids
→ Old screen

PROTOCOL

1. Cut or shred the paper into tiny pieces.

2. Put the paper in a bowl and cover it with water. Soak for 2 hours or overnight.

3. Add the soaked paper to the blender. Mix until it has a smooth, pulpy texture. You may need to add more water as you blend **(fig. 1)**.

4. Divide the paper into small batches, if desired, and add food coloring, glitter, or other decorative material to each batch **(fig. 2)**.

5. Arrange cookie cutters on a screen or make one big piece of paper.

6. Press the pulp into the cookie cutters or press it directly onto the screen **(figs. 3 and 4)**.

7. Flatten the paper with your fingers to squeeze out excess water.

8. Let the paper dry and carefully peel it off the screen **(fig. 5)**.

Fig. 1: Shred, soak, and blend the paper.

Fig. 2: Add food coloring and glitter to small batches of paper.

Fig. 3: Shape the pulp with cookie cutters to make small pieces of paper.

Fig. 4: Press the pulp directly onto the screen to make one large sheet of paper.

CREATIVE ENRICHMENT

→ Use different colors of paper pulp to create a scene, still life, or portrait within the paper itself as you form it on the screen.

→ Make a three-dimensional paper sculpture by molding it over bent screen or wire.

→ Think of different materials you could incorporate into the paper, like cloth, dried leaves or flowers, or even scented oils.

THE STEAM BEHIND THE FUN:

Paper, as we know it today, was first invented in China, between the first and third centuries. Before that, pressed and dried plants such as papyrus, animal skins, bone, bamboo, and even silk were used to write on.

True paper is made from fibers that have been chewed up and re-formed into a flat sheet. It is fairly durable and easy to transport, since it is light and flexible.

Although paper is most often used as a surface for writing, drawing, and painting, paper itself can be made into art, whether by sculpting, folding, cutting it into intricate designs, or tearing and rearranging it to create collages and multimedia art.

Paper engineers combine math, science, and design to create better ways to synthesize, manufacture, and utilize paper products.

HOT GLUE CASTING

011101011110101010101010 0 01011111 0 1010 00000 1000 0 0001 0 1011 11

Create castings from small objects using a glue gun and some playdough.

Fig. 4: Does it look like the original object?

Fig. 1: Press a shell or other small object into some clay or playdough.

Fig. 2: Fill the imprint with hot glue.

Fig. 3: Once the glue hardens, remove it from the playdough and clean it off.

MATERIALS

→ Shells and other objects for making small imprints
→ Clay or playdough
→ Glue gun and glue sticks (colorful glue sticks, if you have them)
→ Scissors

CREATIVE ENRICHMENT

→ Create a piece of art using the shell castings you made.

PROTOCOL

1. Press a shell or another small object into clay or playdough to make an imprint **(fig. 1)**.

2. Fill the imprint with hot glue. Try to get the glue into every nook and cranny **(fig. 2)**.

3. Let the glue cool to room temperature to harden.

4. Remove the glue casting from the clay or playdough and clean it off **(fig. 3)**.

5. Use scissors to cut off any extra glue.

6. Compare the castings to the original objects. Do they look the same **(fig. 4)**?

THE STEAM BEHIND THE FUN:

The process of casting involves pouring a liquid material into a hollow form and letting it harden. Once solidified, the three-dimensional hardened form, also known as a *casting*, is removed from the form. This process is used to mold metal, plaster, concrete, and other materials into complicated forms.

Bronze is made mostly of copper, with some tin or other metals added to make it stronger. Sculptures have been cast in bronze for thousands of years. It can be cast in hollow forms imprinted in sand or in molds made using wax or latex. While some of the most intricate ancient bronzes hail from Nigeria, one of the oldest bronze statues, called "Dancing Girl," was discovered in modern-day Pakistan.

The famous French sculptor Auguste Rodin and his protégé, sculptor Camille Claudel, created bronze sculptures from plaster casts using sand.

FROZEN FLOWERS

01110101111010101010100010111101010000010000000010101111

SAFETY TIPS AND HINTS

→ Adults should supervise young children around open containers of water.

Capture the beauty of blossoms trapped in ice.

Fig. 6: Print the photographs.

MATERIALS

→ Fresh flowers and plants
→ Large, clear plastic containers
→ Water
→ A freezer with empty space
→ Camera
→ Printer

PROTOCOL

1. Cut or pick fresh flowers. Be sure to ask first **(fig. 1)**!

2. Arrange the flowers in a clear, freezable container **(fig. 2)**.

3. Cover the flowers with water and freeze them. You may want to submerge some flowers and leave others sticking out of the water to see what happens **(fig. 3)**.

4. When the water has frozen solid, remove the block of ice from the freezer. You may want to rinse the ice with water at some point to make it clear or remove the block of ice from the container **(fig. 4)**.

5. Take photographs of the flowers from several angles and distances **(fig. 5)**.

6. Keep taking photographs as the ice thaws to see how the flowers change.

7. Print the photographs **(fig. 6)**.

Fig. 1: Cut fresh flowers.

Fig. 2: Put them into a clear container.

Fig. 3: Cover them with water and freeze them.

Fig. 4: Remove the frozen flowers from the freezer and observe them.

Fig. 5: Take photographs from different angles and distances.

Artists like to make viewers see things in a new way. Frozen flowers create thought-provoking images. They may be clearly visible in places and obscured by bubbles and tiny cracks in others. While the flowers trapped in ice remain perfect and unchanged, the ones sticking out of the ice may be wilted or brown in contrast.

The lattice of frozen water keeps air away, preventing color changes caused by chemical reactions.

CREATIVE ENRICHMENT

→ Search online for photographs of frozen flowers created by artists from around the world.
→ Try freezing other objects in an interesting way and photographing them. For example, cut apart an apple and freeze it next to a whole apple.
→ Freeze flowers inside a water balloon. When the water is frozen, cut off the balloon to reveal the ice sculpture.

LAB 36

FRUIT AND VEGGIE STAMPS

01110101111010101010101010010101111010101000000010000000010101111

SAFETY TIPS AND HINTS

→ Adults should cut fruits such as apples and oranges in half. Let kids cut grapes and strawberries with a plastic knife, if they want to help.

→ Do not eat food that has been dipped in paint.

Use the shapes and patterns in fruits and vegetables to print a masterpiece.

Fig. 3: Try to make a pattern.

MATERIALS

→ **Fruits and veggies, such as apples, grapes, corn, oranges, and peppers**
→ **Plastic knife (for kids) or sharp knife (for adults)**
→ **Cutting board**
→ **Washable paint, like tempera**
→ **Plates**
→ **Paper**

PROTOCOL

1. Halve the fruits and vegetables so you can see the seeds and shapes inside. Divide them vertically and horizontally to compare (**fig. 1**).

2. Spread paint on several plates so there are different colors to choose from (**fig. 2**).

3. Dip the cut fruit and veggies into the paint and use them to make prints on paper.

4. Can you make a pattern (**fig. 3**)?

5. Try to identify which fruit or veggie made which print (**fig. 4**).

Fig. 1: Cut fruits and veggies so you can see their seeds and shapes.

Fig. 2: Spread several colors of paint on plates and make prints.

Fig. 4: Can you identify which fruits or vegetables made each print?

CREATIVE ENRICHMENT

→ You see different types of symmetry depending on how you cut a piece of fruit in half. Cut one apple in half from top to bottom and cut another in half from side to side. Describe what type of symmetry you observe in each (see STEAM Behind the Fun following).

→ Use a small circular fruit, like half a grape, to make a pointillist painting, which is a painting made of lots of dots. Look up pictures online of some pointillist paintings to get ideas.

THE
STEAM
BEHIND THE FUN:

Symmetry is everywhere you look. You'll notice it when you glance in the mirror and compare the two sides of your reflection or when you get a closeup view of a snowflake. The dictionary defines it as "the quality of being made up of exactly similar parts facing each other or around an axis." When you cut a piece of fruit in half, you'll observe a different type of symmetry, depending on whether you divide it from top to bottom or side to side.

There are three main types of symmetry. If something has *reflectional* symmetry, it looks the same on both sides of an imaginary line, like a butterfly. Objects with *rotational* symmetry can be spun around a central point and still look the same, like a starfish. Designs and objects with *point* symmetry have identical matching parts an equal distance from the same point, but in the opposite direction.

SCRATCHBOARD ETCHING

0111010111101010101010010011111010100000010000000010101111

Use highlighters and crayons to create colorful paper to scratch.

Fig. 3: Scratch off the crayon wax to make designs.

PROTOCOL

1. Cover an index card or piece of paper with patches of highlighter in different colors (**fig. 1**).

2. Use a black crayon to create a thick layer of wax over the highlighter colors (**fig. 2**).

3. With the point of a toothpick or wooden skewer, scratch designs into the wax, revealing the colors beneath (**fig. 3**).

4. Use a fine point to make delicate designs or a thicker one for bold lines (**fig. 4**).

SAFETY TIPS AND HINTS

→ Use plenty of black crayon to cover the highlighter.

MATERIALS

→ Index cards or paper
→ Highlighting pens in different colors
→ Black crayon
→ Wooden skewer or toothpick

Fig. 1: Cover paper with highlighter.

Fig. 2: Cover the highlighter colors with black crayon.

Fig. 4: Use a fine point to make delicate lines.

CREATIVE ENRICHMENT

→ Reengineer this project using different materials. Test markers, pastels, watercolors, and paint to see which materials provide the best result.
→ Cut a potato in half and use a skewer to make grooves on the flat part. Coat the potato with a thin layer of paint and use it to stamp a piece of paper, creating a negative print, where the lines you carved look white against the paint from the potato.

THE STEAM BEHIND THE FUN:

Traditional etching is done on wax-coated metal plates, which are processed to create prints on paper. Artists begin the process by scratching designs into the wax. When the design is complete, the coated plate is dipped in acid, which eats away the bare metal underneath, creating grooves where the wax has been scratched away.

The plate is removed from the acid and the rest of the wax is removed. When the artist is ready to print, the metal plate is coated with ink. Excess ink is wiped off, but some ink remains in the grooves. The metal plate is put in a machine called a *printing press*, which pushes paper down on the plate, allowing it to pick up ink from the etched lines. Many prints can be made using the same plate.

BOLD BATIKS

`0 1 1 1 0 1 0 1 1 1 1 0 1 0 1 0 1 0 1 0 1 0 1 0 0 1 0 1 0 1 1 1 1 1 0 1 0 1 0 0 0 0 0 0 0 1 0 0 0 0 0 0 0 0 1 0 1 0 1 1 1 1`

SAFETY TIPS AND HINTS

→ Adults should supervise young children around open containers of water. If you use a blow dryer, keep it away from water.

Create beautiful designs using glue and paint.

Fig. 5: Show off your design.

MATERIALS

→ White glue
→ White cotton fabric, such as dishtowels
→ Blow dryer (optional)
→ Washable paint, like tempera
→ Paintbrushes
→ Plastic container

PROTOCOL

1. Use glue to make designs on fabric (**fig. 1**).

2. Let the glue dry. (You can speed this up using a blow dryer.)

3. When the glue is dry, use bright colors to paint designs over the glue (**fig. 2**).

4. Let the paint dry (**fig. 3**).

5. When the paint is dry, wash out the excess paint from the fabric with water (**fig. 4**).

6. Scrape off any remaining glue and let your masterpiece dry.

7. Show off your design (**fig. 5**).

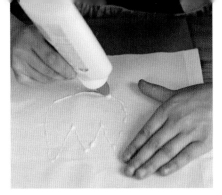

Fig. 1: Use glue to make designs on fabric.

Fig. 2: When the glue is dry, paint designs over it.

Fig. 4: Wash out excess paint with water.

Fig. 3: Let the paint dry.

CREATIVE ENRICHMENT

→ Think of other things you could use as a water- and paint-resistant material. Try making batiks using wax from crayons or rubber cement.
→ Use batik to decorate a piece of cloth with a pattern of interconnected geometric shapes (see Lab 47, page 124).

THE
STEAM
BEHIND THE FUN:

The word *hydrophobic* means "water fearing." Hydrophobic materials such as wax repel water. If you paint or drip hot wax onto fabric, it protects the fibers from bonding with dyes.

Since ancient times, people have been using wax to help create designs on fabric. Batik uses water-resistant materials to create designs on fabric. The method is used in many countries around the world, but some of the most well-known batik art is produced on the island of Java, in Indonesia.

EMBOSSING

`0 1 1 1 0 1 0 1 1 1 1 0 1 0 1 0 1 0 1 0 1 0 0 1 0 1 1 1 1 0 1 0 1 0 0 0 0 0 0 1 0 0 0 0 0 0 0 0 1 0 1 0 1 1 1 1`

SAFETY TIPS AND HINTS

→ Push hard on the cardstock with the pen or stylus to get a good impression.

→ We use a stencil here for part of the lab, which is a design cut out of thick paper or cardboard. If you don't have a stencil, you can make your own using thick paper and a cutting tool.

Decorate card stock or aluminum foil with raised designs and patterns.

Fig. 2: Position card stock or thick paper over the stencil, tape it down, and trace the shapes.

MATERIALS

→ Stencil
→ Tape
→ Card stock or very thick paper like watercolor paper
→ Retractable ballpoint pen or stylus
→ Heavy-duty aluminum foil
→ Plastic container
→ Toothpick or wooden skewer

PROTOCOL

1. Tape a stencil to a window (fig. 1).

2. Position card stock or thick paper over the stencil and tape it down.

3. Use the end of a ballpoint pen with the tip retracted or a stylus to trace the edges of the stencil designs. Push hard against the paper (fig. 2)!

4. Remove the paper from the window and flip it over to see the embossed designs (fig. 3).

5. To emboss foil, stretch a piece of heavy-duty foil over the open top of a plastic container.

6. Use a toothpick or stylus to draw gently on the foil. If you push too hard, the point will break through (fig. 4).

7. Remove the foil and flip it over to see the embossed design (fig. 5).

Fig. 1: Tape the stencil to a window.

Fig. 3: Remove the paper to see the embossed designs.

Fig. 4: You can emboss images on foil, too.

Fig. 5: Flip the foil over to see the embossed design.

CREATIVE ENRICHMENT

→ Try embossing other materials or different kinds of paper. What works best?

THE
STEAM
BEHIND THE FUN:

Embossing is the process of creating raised patterns or designs on a surface. The technique has traditionally been used to make stamps and ornate seals on letters or to authenticate documents. Professional embossers use machines to stamp images onto paper. The machine contains two metal pieces called *dies*. When a piece of paper is squeezed between the two parts, the die with the raised design pushes paper into the imprint of the other die—embossing it.

Because paper can be pressed, folded, and molded from two dimensions into three, many artists use it as a medium for art. While some cubists incorporated newspaper into their work, many modern artists use traditional methods alongside technology to print, cut, and sculpt paper into intricate forms and lifelike masterpieces.

MIRROR-IMAGE PLANT PRINTS

01110101111010101010101010010101111101010100000001000000001010111

SAFETY TIPS AND HINTS

→ Protective eyewear is recommended. Young children should have adult supervision when using mallets and hammers.

→ **If pretreating your cloth:** The day before you want to do the project, add 2 quarts (1.9 L) of water to a large pot. Add 1 tablespoon (12 g) of alum and 1 teaspoon of baking soda to the water. Add the cloth and bring to a boil. Simmer for 2 hours, turn off the heat, and soak the cloth for at least 2 hours. Let the cloth dry before proceeding.

Use a hammer or mallet to transfer plant pigments to cloth, creating beautiful prints of your favorite leaves and flowers.

Fig. 6: You've created a mirror image!

MATERIALS

→ Alum and baking soda to treat cloth (optional; I don't pretreat my fabric, but the treatment step will help bond and preserve color. You can also buy fabric that's pretreated for dyeing. See Safety Tips and Hints.)
→ Untextured cotton cloth, such as a dishtowel (heavy cloth works better than very thin cloth)
→ Fresh leaves and flowers (dried leaves won't work)
→ Hard, smooth pounding surface, such as a wooden cutting board or carving board
→ Wax paper or plastic wrap
→ Protective glasses

→ Iron and ironing surface
→ Mallets or hammers

PROTOCOL

1. Take a walk to collect colorful leaves and flowers. Choose plants that can be flattened **(fig. 1)**. Flowers with huge centers, like coneflowers, don't work as well, but their petals may be removed and pounded.

2. Cover the pounding surface with wax paper or plastic wrap.

3. Cut a piece of cloth to fit on the pounding surface when it's folded in half. Iron the fold.

4. Open the cloth and lay it on the pounding surface.

5. Arrange leaves and flowers on one half (side) of the cloth **(fig. 2)**.

6. Fold the other half (side) of the cloth over the plants. Put on your protective glasses and pound the cloth with the hammer or mallet. If you're using a hammer, pound gently **(figs. 3 and 4)**.

Fig. 1: Collect leaves and flowers.

Fig. 2: Arrange the plants on the cloth.

Fig. 3: Fold the cloth over the plants.

Fig. 4: Pound the cloth with a hammer or mallet.

Fig. 5: Unfold the cloth to reveal the prints.

7. Pound until you can see the forms of the leaves through the fabric. As the pigment leaks through, you'll see the outlines of what you're smashing. *Hint: Hammers work better than mallets for fall leaves. For juicy leaves and flowers, use the mallet or hammer gently.*

8. When you're finished pounding, unfold the fabric to reveal the print you created. Remove the leaves and petals **(fig. 5 and 6)**.

9. Label the image with plant names, enhance it with paint or markers, or leave nature's design to speak for itself.

CREATIVE ENRICHMENT

→ What parts of the leaf can you identify in the print you created?

THE
STEAM
BEHIND THE FUN:

Flowers, leave, fruits, and vegetables are full of brilliant pigments that give them color. In this experiment, we transfer plant pigments to cloth using pressure from a hammer or mallet.

The green pigment found in leaves is called *chlorophyll*. In the fall, many trees stop making chlorophyll and the red, yellow, and orange pigments inside the leaves become visible.

The color may be more intense on one side of the print. A waxy covering called a *cuticle* covers leaves and is sometimes thicker on the top than on the underside of the leaf.

NAIL POLISH-MARBLED EGGS

LAB 41

SAFETY TIPS AND HINTS

→ Removing egg yolks can be tricky. An adult or older sibling will need to help young children.

→ Adult supervision is required when using nail polish or pushpins.

→ Creating marbled eggs takes practice and patience. Don't get frustrated. You have to work fast, before the nail polish dries on the water. Some colors will work better than others.

Create gorgeous swirling designs on hollow eggs.

Fig. 5: Try to create different patterns.

MATERIALS
→ 12 raw white eggs
→ Pushpin
→ Paper clip
→ Syringe or egg-blower tool for removing egg whites and yolk
→ Disposable gloves, like latex or nitrile
→ Small disposable container
→ Water
→ Nail polish (several colors)
→ Toothpicks

PROTOCOL

1. Use a pushpin to poke a hole in each end of a raw egg.

2. Unbend a paper clip, insert one end through the pinhole into the egg, and use it to "scramble" the egg, breaking the yolk.

3. Fill the syringe with air. Insert it into the egg and force the egg out of the pinhole at the opposite end. When the egg is empty, rinse it with water and dry it. Repeat with all the eggs **(fig. 1)**.

4. Put gloves on and fill a small disposable container with water.

5. Shake up the nail polish and loosen the lids.

6. Put a drop of nail polish in the water.

7. Quickly add another drop or two to the center of the polish you already added **(fig. 2)**.

8. Immediately use a toothpick to make designs in the polish.

Fig. 1: Poke holes in each end of a raw egg and remove the yolk and white.

Fig. 2: Drip nail polish into a disposable container full of water.

Fig. 3: Roll the egg in the polish design to cover with a single layer of polish.

Fig. 4: It may take some practice.

9. Roll an egg over the nail polish design, trying to layer it on the egg smoothly **(fig. 3)**.

10. Use a toothpick to remove excess polish from the container and repeat with the other side of the same egg or a new egg **(fig. 4)**.

11. Create lots of patterns **(fig. 5)**.

CREATIVE ENRICHMENT

→ To marble fingernails, cover the skin around your nails with tape or petroleum jelly. Add polish to the water and lift the design onto your nails **(fig. 6)**.

Fig. 6: Put tape or petroleum jelly on your fingers to marble your nails.

THE
STEAM
BEHIND THE FUN:

Nail polish floats on water because it's less dense than water. The polish contains chemicals that help it dry quickly, which is good when you paint it on fingernails, but makes this lab a little trickier.

Most cosmetics are created by scientists and engineers. Safety, shelf life, brilliant color, fragrance, and smooth application all depend on getting the right mix of chemicals. From nail polish to lipsticks and lotion, chemistry rules.

π
UNIT
05
MATH

MOST PEOPLE THINK OF MATHEMATICS AS A METHOD OF CALCULATION. IN FACT, MATH IS A SOURCE OF ENORMOUS INSPIRATION FOR CONCEPTS THAT CAN BE APPLIED TO ART, ENGINEERING, PHYSICS, TECHNOLOGY, MEDICINE, AND MUSIC— TO NAME ONLY A FEW.

Almost everything in the universe can be described by mathematical equation, and once something has been described by math, it's only a matter of time until someone finds ways to apply it to a question or a problem.

For example, the Ancient Greeks came up with the concept of the atom by thinking about number sequences and fractions. Once you start dividing something, like an apple, it gets smaller and smaller: $\frac{1}{2}$, $\frac{1}{4}$, $\frac{1}{8}$, $\frac{1}{16}$, $\frac{1}{32}$, $\frac{1}{64}$, and so on. Do you see the pattern? Each number in the denominator is twice the number in the previous fraction, and the Greeks imagined that, at some point, you would create a piece so tiny it couldn't be divided any more. The Greek philosopher Democritus described this "uncuttable," or "atomos," piece of matter as an "atom."

In this unit, you'll make a Möbius strip, cut up apples to learn about fractions, try your hand at creating cubist art, play with patterns and fractals, and draw a Fibonacci spiral.

> *"When I'm not making music, I'm doing tech stuff at my day job. And half the time when I am making music, I'm doing tech stuff, too. In the meantime, all the logic I picked up in math classes and in the programming I've done is constantly echoing and bleeding into all the problem solving that is songwriting, arranging, and recording. Art, science, math, music, design, chemistry, emotions, biology. It's all one thing."*
> —*Matt Wilson, singer-songwriter and producer with the bands Trip Shakespeare and The Twilight Hours*

CUBIST CREATIONS

SAFETY TIPS AND HINTS

→ Let your imagination go wild!

Cubist artists were interested in showing objects in new ways, often drawing them from several angles or perspectives at the same time, in an attempt to capture their essence rather than create an exact replica. Here, we'll rearrange the geometric shapes you find in animals to make cubist art.

Fig. 3: Re-create your design in sculpting clay.

MATERIALS

→ Printer or magazine with photos of animals
→ Scissors
→ Pencil
→ Markers or paint
→ Paper
→ Sculpting material such as clay or playdough

PROTOCOL

1. Print out a photograph of an animal or cut one out of a magazine **(fig. 1)**.

2. Find the geometric shapes in the animal, like circles, ovals, triangles, rectangles, and squares.

3. Use markers to draw the same shapes on another piece of paper, but reorganize them. Try to arrange them in a way that represents something about how the animal behaves, or how it hunts, or how it moves. You can change the size of the shapes **(fig. 2)**.

4. Re-create the original animal and the reconstructed one you drew using sculpting material **(figs. 3 and 4)**.

Fig. 1: Print out a photo of an animal and find geometric shapes.

Fig. 2: Draw the shapes in a different order.

Fig. 4: Be creative!

Fig. 5: Can you still recognize the animal?

5. Draw or paint a second cubist animal. This time, look at the sculpted forms you made and draw the shapes you see as though you're looking at them from more than one angle at the same time **(fig. 5)**.

CREATIVE ENRICHMENT

→ Make a cubist collage of the animal, incorporating paper and textiles that say something about the animal or seem interesting.
→ Look up a recipe online for conductive playdough and use it to create cubist playdough animals that can light an LED.

THE
STEAM
BEHIND THE FUN:

While geometric shapes, like squares and triangles, tend to have symmetry and hard lines, biometric shapes are curved, irregular, and frequently found in nature. Great artists are very good at finding shapes and using them to make their work more interesting and effective.

Representational art makes things look more or less the way we expect them to look, although it uses color and technique to emphasize certain elements.

Cubism arrived in Europe in the early twentieth century, turning representational art on its head. Artists exploring cubism made paintings and collages that presented subject matter as geometric shapes.

PATTERN STYLE

`0111010111101010101010101010010101111010100000001000000010101111`

Tape together some fashion-forward fun.

Fig. 5: What else could you create?

MATERIALS
→ Duct tape (2 or more colors)
→ Scissors
→ Key chain loop or jewelry hardware (optional)

PROTOCOL

1. Tear off a square of duct tape. Fold two corners to the middle to create a triangle **(fig. 1)**.

2. Smooth the tape down **(fig. 2)**.

3. Create another tape triangle (in a different color). Put one triangle sticky-side down and put another one on top of it, pointing in the same direction, so the one below sticks out by about ¼ inch (6 mm). The tape will make them stick together.

4. Repeat with several more triangles, creating repeating patterns **(fig. 3)**.

5. When your pattern is complete, trim the sides and use the tape art to create a bookmark, keychain, earrings, or other item **(fig. 4)**.

6. If you don't have pierced ears, use a piece of tape to attach the earrings.

7. What else could you make **(fig. 5)**?

Fig. 1: Tear off a square of duct tape. Fold two corners down to the middle.

Fig. 2: Smooth the tape.

Fig. 3: Tape triangles to form a repeating pattern.

Fig. 4: When you're done, trim the sides and create bookmarks and accessories.

CREATIVE ENRICHMENT

→ Invent a new way to fold duct tape to create an original design.

THE
STEAM
BEHIND THE FUN:

Patterns are repeated forms that can be found both in nature and in things we make. We incorporate them into everything from music to architecture.

To create camouflage, designers either create mimicking patterns allowing objects to blend in to a particular background or they create disruptive patterns where any regular patterns have been destroyed.

In math, sequences are strings of numbers that follow a pattern. You'll find them in multiplication tables and in more complex numerical patterns, like the Fibonacci sequence (see Lab 46, page 122).

Ada Lovelace was the first mathematician to see the enormous potential of computers. Perhaps some of the inspiration for this idea came from her familiarity with patterns in art. In 1843, she said, "The Analytical Engine weaves algebraic patterns just as the Jacquard loom weaves flowers and leaves."

FRACTAL GEOMETRY

SAFETY TIPS AND HINTS

→ For young children, it may help to draw an example for them to follow. Let them take it from there!

Repeat a simple shape to create a beautiful, branching tree.

Fig. 4: Add color to your drawing.

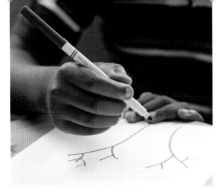

Fig. 1: Draw 2 or 3 large Y shapes to create a tree trunk.

Fig. 2: Branch out with smaller and smaller Ys.

MATERIALS
→ Paper
→ Pencil or pen
→ Paint (optional)

PROTOCOL

1. Draw 2 or 3 large Y shapes on a piece of paper to form the trunk of a tree **(fig. 1)**.

2. Create new branches extending from the first ones by drawing more, smaller Y shapes **(fig. 2)**.

3. Keep going until your tree has branched out into tiny twigs at the perimeter **(fig. 3)**.

4. Add some color and details to your drawing to bring the tree to life **(fig. 4)**.

Fig. 3: Create smaller and smaller branches.

CREATIVE ENRICHMENT
→ Look up more complicated fractals to draw. For example, you can draw a Koch snowflake using triangles.

THE STEAM
BEHIND THE FUN:

Some shapes on earth have a strange property, where if you divide them, each part looks like the whole, but smaller. These repeating shapes are called *fractals*. In nature, you find them everywhere, from tree branches and the bronchi in your lungs to cauliflower florets and the arms of a snowflake. Human-made fractal patterns are found around the world. In Africa, many villages, art, and even fences display fractal patterns.

The mathematician Benoit Mandelbrot coined the term *fractal*. He studied what he called "roughness" and "self-similarity" in nature and used math to describe fractals. His discoveries have been used in the stock market, medicine, and movie technology, among other things. He's most famous for discovering the Mandelbrot Set, which is a set of numbers defining an infinitely complicated fractal boundary.

PERSPECTIVE PAINTING

01110101111010101010101010 0 01011111010100000001000000001010111

SAFETY TIPS AND HINTS

→ For inspiration, look at some images of roads and receding landscapes before you begin. Check out Vincent van Gogh's masterpiece *The Bedroom* and Berthe Morisot's painting *The Harbor at Lorient* for ideas. What tricks do the artists use to make things appear close up or far away?

Divide paper into four similar triangles, with an imaginary vanishing point at the center to create the illusion of distance.

Fig. 4: Add lots of color and detail to your painting.

MATERIALS

→ Ruler
→ Pencil
→ A square piece of paper or canvas, any size
→ Eraser
→ Paint or markers

PROTOCOL

1. Use a ruler to guide you as you draw diagonal lines from corner to corner on a square piece of paper.

2. Draw a small dot where the lines meet in the center. This dot is the vanishing point, where everything will recede away into the distance in the scene you're about to draw.

3. If you're making a room, draw a square in the center of the canvas to represent the back wall. Draw a door in the wall (**figs. 1 and 2**).

4. If you're drawing a road receding into the distance, draw a triangle from the vanishing point at the middle of the painting to the center of the bottom of the painting. Make it wider as it gets farther from the vanishing point and closer to the bottom of the page. (**fig. 3**).

5. Use a pencil to add detail to your drawing, and an eraser to erase any mistakes. Objects near the edge of the page should be bigger and they should get smaller and smaller as they approach the vanishing point in the center. Use lots of lines that are parallel to the sides of your paper or to the diagonal lines you drew on the page.

Fig. 1: Use a ruler to guide you as you draw.

Fig. 2: Draw a room by creating a square in the center with a door in the middle.

Fig. 3: Or, make a road disappear into the distance.

6. If you drew a room, try adding a painting or two to the walls of your drawing, keeping them in perspective, too.

7. Add color to your perspective drawing using paint or markers **(fig. 4)**.

CREATIVE ENRICHMENT

→ Create another perspective painting of a room on a large piece of paper. Can you use one of the paintings on the wall to draw a room within a room? Don't forget to use perspective in the miniature room, too!

THE STEAM BEHIND THE FUN:

Perspective is the art of using math and geometry to make three-dimensional things look real on a two-dimensional surface, like a piece of paper.

Single-point perspective drawings contain a single vanishing point on the horizon and are good for representing things directly facing the viewer, like a hallway, a room, or a road going off into the distance.

Objects that are farther away look smaller as the result of the angle of the light hitting our eyes. When something is close to you, light bounces off it and into your eyes at a steep angle, but the farther away an object is, the shallower the angle becomes and the smaller it looks.

In this lab, we divide our paper into four similar triangles, with an imaginary vanishing point at the center. The vanishing point represents the angle at which you could no longer see an object.

FIBONACCI SPIRAL

`0 1 1 1 0 1 0 1 1 1 1 0 1 0 1 0 1 0 1 0 1 0 0 0 1 0 1 1 1 1 0 1 0 1 0 0 0 0 0 0 1 0 0 0 0 0 0 0 1 0 1 0 1 1 1`

SAFETY TIPS AND HINTS

→ Using a compass takes practice. Don't get frustrated!

→ Start by writing the Fibonacci sequence, so you'll know how big to make your squares. Just add each number in the sequence to the previous one to get the next number: 1, 1, 2, 3, 5, 8, 13, 21, 34, 55, and so on.

Create a perfect spiral using mathematics.

Fig. 4: You've drawn a Fibonacci spiral.

MATERIALS
→ **Large piece of paper, at least 15 inches x 22 inches (38 x 55 cm) or tape together pieces of paper to create 1 large sheet**
→ **Pencil**
→ **Ruler or yardstick (meter stick)**
→ **Compass**

PROTOCOL
1. Orient your paper in a horizontal position.

2. Use a ruler to measure and draw two adjacent ½ x ½ inch (1 x 1 cm) squares. Place the squares approximately 7 inches (18 cm) from the left side and 4¾ inches (12 cm) down from the top of the paper **(fig. 1)**.

3. Add an adjacent ¾ x ¾ inch (2 x 2 cm) square directly below the first two squares **(fig. 2)**.

4. Draw a 1¼ inch (3 cm) square to the right of the previous squares.

5. Add a 2 inch (5 cm) square above the other squares.

6. Draw a 3 inch (7.5 cm) square to the left, a 5 inch (13 cm) square below that, and, finally, an 8½ inch (21 cm) square on the right of everything.

7. Use your compass to draw connecting arcs in the ½ inch (1 cm) squares on the right by placing the compass point on the connecting point at the bottom of the two squares and the pencil on the lower right corner before sweeping it to the left to create a semicircle.

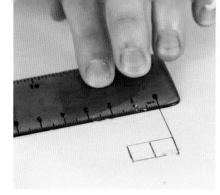

Fig. 1: Draw two adjacent ½ x-½ inch (1 x 1 cm) squares.

Fig. 2: Add adjacent ¾ inch (2 cm) squares, 1¼ inch (3 cm), 2 inch (5 cm), and 3 inch (8 cm) squares.

8. Put the compass point on the upper right-hand corner of the ¾ inch (2 cm) square and continue the arched line.

9. Use the compass to connect all the squares with an unbroken curved line until you've created a spiral that runs through all the squares **(figs. 3 and 4)**.

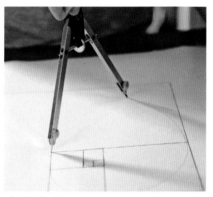

Fig. 3: Use a compass to draw connecting arcs in each square.

CREATIVE ENRICHMENT

→ Look up images of Fibonacci spirals in nature and decorate your spiral to look like one of them **(figs. 5 and 6)**.

Fig. 5: Turn your spiral into a natural design.

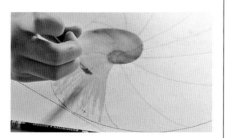

Fig. 6: Add some color to your design.

THE STEAM
BEHIND THE FUN:

The Fibonacci sequence is a series of numbers, where every number is the sum of the two proceeding numbers. For example, 1 + 1 = 2, 1 + 2 = 3, 2 + 3 = 5, 3 + 5 = 8, and so on. You end up with the sequence (1, 1, 2, 3, 5, 8, 13, 21, 34, 55 . . .).

A Fibonacci spiral is created by making an array of squares using Fibonacci dimensions and connecting them using quarter circles. Fibonacci numbers and spirals appear frequently in nature, in everything from sunflower seed patterns and hurricanes to far-away galaxies.

If you divide a number in the Fibonacci sequence by the previous one, you'll get a number close to 1.618, which is known as *the golden ratio*, or *phi*. Many artists have used this ratio to compose spaces and faces in their work, and the golden ratios found in the first seven numbers of the Fibonacci series are related to the vibrational frequency of musical notes.

TESSELLATIONS

`0 1 1 1 0 1 0 1 1 1 1 0 1 0 1 0 1 0 1 0 1 0 0 0 1 0 1 1 1 1 0 1 0 1 0 0 0 0 0 0 1 0 0 0 0 0 0 0 1 0 1 0 1 1 1`

SAFETY TIPS AND HINTS

→ Adult supervision is required when using a glue gun.

Tile poster board with gum or pasta to create a mathematical mosaic.

Fig. 5: Try to fill in all the empty space.

MATERIALS

→ Several packs of gum (optional)
→ Pasta, bow tie and penne work well (optional)
→ Glue (school glue or a glue gun and glue sticks)
→ Sturdy paper surface, such as poster board or foam-core board

PROTOCOL

1. If making a gum tessellation, decide whether to use wrapped or unwrapped gum.

2. Start in one corner of the board's surface and use glue to create a tightly interlocking, repeating pattern of gum or pasta. Unwrapped gum makes your art project smell great **(figs. 1, 2, and 3)**!

3. Keep gluing gum or pasta on the board until it's completely covered **(figs. 4 and 5)**.

4. Try using different, interlocking pasta shapes.

5. How many different patterns can you create?

Fig. 1: Glue gum to the poster board in repeating patterns that cover the paper.

Fig. 2: Try doing the same thing using pasta.

Fig. 3: Unwrapped gum makes your art smell good.

Fig. 4: Create patterns as you go.

CREATIVE ENRICHMENT

→ Look online for some tessellations created by M. C. Escher.
→ Find other shapes you could use to make tessellations or find an item to trace and use it to draw tessellations. You could also create a new form to use for making tessellated patterns.

THE STEAM
BEHIND THE FUN:

Tessellations are patterns made up of shapes that fit together perfectly, leaving no blank space between them. Tessellation is also called *tiling*. If you completely cover a flat surface with squares, equilateral triangles, or hexagons that all join up in the same way, you've created a regular tessellation.

In nature, you can see regular tessellation in the honeycombs created by bees. Crystals are three-dimensional molecular tessellations, formed by repeated patterns filling space.

Since the time of the Ancient Sumerians, tiny geometric shapes have been used to create mosaics from clay, stone, and glass tiles. Some of the most beautiful mosaics in the world have been created by cultures where energy has been focused on creating complicated geometric patterns. The artist M.C. Escher was famous for his creative tessellations.

SERIAL DILUTIONS

SAFETY TIPS AND HINTS

→ This is a great project to do at snack time. Don't waste the milk and cereal. Eat it!

Use cereal and food coloring to learn a laboratory technique.

Fig. 2: Mix and scoop a spoonful of cereal to the next cup. Repeat 3 more times.

MATERIALS

→ 2½ cups (570 ml) milk
→ 5 clear plastic cups or small cereal bowls
→ ¼ cup (weight varies) breakfast cereal
→ 5 cups (1.2 L) water
→ Food coloring
→ Measuring spoons
→ Measuring cups

PROTOCOL

1. Add ½ cup (120 ml) of milk to each of the five cups.

2. Add the cereal to the first cup (fig. 1).

3. Mix the cereal and milk in the cup. Take a spoonful of milk and cereal out of the first cup to put it into the second cup.

4. Mix up the milk and cereal in the second cup and repeat—taking a spoonful of mixed up milk and cereal to put in the next cup in line (fig. 2).

5. Compare how many pieces of cereal are in each cup.

6. Eat the cereal and wash the cups to reuse.

7. For the second part of the experiment, add 1 cup (235 ml) of water to each cup.

8. To the first cup, add several drops of food coloring and stir (fig. 3).

9. To make a 1 to 10 dilution, measure 5 teaspoons (25 ml) of colored water and add it to the second cup (fig. 4).

Fig. 1: Add ½ cup (120 ml) of milk to each of the five cups. Add cereal to the first cup.

Fig. 3: Add 1 cup (235 ml) of water to each of the five cups and add food coloring to the first cup.

Fig. 4: Add 5 teaspoons (25 ml) of colored water to the second cup.

10. To make a 1 to 100 dilution, take 5 teaspoons (25 ml) of colored water from the second cup and put it in the third cup and so on. Repeat until you have diluted colored water in all the cups.

11. Congratulations! You've made serial dilutions **(fig. 5)**.

Cup 1 = undiluted
Cup 2 = 1 to 10 dilution
Cup 3 = 1 to 100 dilution
Cup 4 = 1 to 1,000 dilution
Cup 5 = 1 to 10,000 dilution

Fig. 5: You've made 1:10 serial dilutions!

THE STEAM BEHIND THE FUN:

Serial dilutions are often used in scientific laboratories to quickly and accurately decrease the concentration of chemicals or microbes in liquid.

In the breakfast cereal portion of this lab, each time you dilute the milk/cereal mixture, you end up with fewer and fewer pieces of cereal in the milk.

Food coloring molecules are much smaller than cereal, but when you do serial dilutions of food coloring in water, the same thing happens. You end up with fewer food coloring molecules in each cup. The more dilutions you do, the lighter the color becomes.

CREATIVE ENRICHMENT

→ Instead of adding plain water, add water containing a color, like yellow, to each cup. Do serial dilutions with another color to see how color mixing works with different dilutions.

MATH-TOOL ART

SAFETY TIPS AND HINTS

→ Protractors have sharp points, so younger children should use them under adult supervision.

Practice using math tools and transform your lines, circles, and arcs into a work of art.

Fig. 4: Use color to enhance the shapes and lines you created.

MATERIALS

→ Pencil
→ Ruler
→ Paper
→ Protractor
→ Compass
→ Markers
→ Paint

PROTOCOL

1. Practice drawing straight lines with a ruler. Draw some parallel lines and use the ruler to make some squares, triangles, and other polygons **(fig. 1)**.

2. Trace a protractor. Mark some angles and use a ruler to draw them.

3. Try to make a circle with a compass. It can take some practice **(fig. 2)**!

4. Turn the lines and shapes you created into a piece of art. Be creative **(fig. 3)**!

5. Add color to your mathematical masterpiece **(fig. 4)**.

Fig. 1: Use math tools like rulers, compasses, and protractors to make a design.

Fig. 2: Using a compass can take practice!

Fig. 3: Be creative with your mathematical art!

CREATIVE ENRICHMENT

→ Make a giant compass in the driveway using a string (or jump rope) and a piece of chalk. Have one person stand in the middle holding the string. Tie the chalk to the other end and draw a giant circle. Pull the string straight and use it to draw a hopscotch grid.

→ Use a compass to draw flower petals on paper or the driveway. Use the drawing of the fan blade design in Lab 18 (Wind Turbine, see page 52) as a starting point.

THE STEAM BEHIND THE FUN:

Ancient Greek mathematicians employed a method called *classical construction* to draw angles and geometric figures using only a compass and a straight edge, which is a ruler without markings. Although they were able to draw a number of shapes and angles with great accuracy using this technique, there were some thing they couldn't do with these simple tools.

Today, computers and drawing programs are used for much of the precision drawing done by mathematicians, engineers, architects, and artists. However, you'll use tools that include rulers, compasses, and protractors for the math you will encounter in school, so it's good to get acquainted with them.

MÖBIUS STRIP MOBILE

`011101011110101010101010010101111101010000001000000001010111`

Engineer a mobile using two-sided paper strips twisted into odd, single-surface loops.

Fig. 5: Hang it to display.

MATERIALS

→ Paper or card stock
→ Scissors
→ Markers, crayons, or paint
→ Tape
→ Straws (the paper kind work best)
→ String or fishing line
→ Paper clips

PROTOCOL

1. Cut some strips of paper around ⅔ inch (1.5 cm) wide and 6 inches (15 cm) long. Once you get the hang of making Möbius strips, you can cut paper strips of any dimension.

2. If the paper is white, add some color or design to the strips.

3. Make each paper strip into a loop. Flip one of the ends over and tape the ends together. You may need to work the paper with your fingers to smooth out any bends. This odd twisted loop is called a *Möbius strip* **(fig. 1)**.

4. Make several more Möbius strips for the mobile.

5. For fun, make a white Möbius strip. Using a marker, start drawing a line around the strip. Without lifting your pen, you will end up in the same spot where you started!

6. Tape two straws together as a perpendicular cross to create a mobile frame **(fig. 2)**.

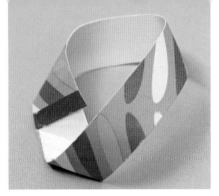

Fig. 1: Cut thin strips of paper and tape opposite sides of the ends together to form twisted loops.

Fig. 2: Tape two straws together to create a mobile frame.

Fig. 3: Attach the Möbius strips to the frame using paper clips and fishing line.

Fig. 4: Balance the mobile.

7. Attach the Möbius strips to the frame using paper clips and fishing line **(fig. 3)**.

8. Balance the mobile and find a place to hang it **(figs. 4 and 5)**.

CREATIVE ENRICHMENT

→ Make a large Möbius strip and cut it down the center line. What happens?
→ Make a Möbius strip and attempt to draw it from several angles. If it's casting a shadow, draw the shadow, too.

FRUIT FRACTION ANIMALS

`0 1 1 1 0 1 0 1 1 1 1 0 1 0 1 0 1 0 1 0 1 0 1 0 0 1 0 1 1 1 1 1 0 1 0 1 0 0 0 0 0 0 1 0 0 0 0 0 0 0 1 0 1 0 1 1 1 1`

SAFETY TIPS AND HINTS

→ Adult supervision is required for cutting.

Learn about fractions and eat your creative math project.

Fig. 5: What else could you create?

MATERIALS

→ Paring knife or plastic cutting knife
→ Fresh fruit
→ Cutting board
→ Toothpicks

PROTOCOL

1. Use a paring knife to cut a piece of fruit in half or use a plastic knife if the fruit is soft **(fig. 1)**.

Fig. 1: Cut a piece of fruit in half.

Fig. 2: Cut it in half again to make quarters.

Fig. 3: Cut other fruit into fractions.

Fig. 4: Use toothpicks to create creatures from the fruit fractions.

2. Cut the same piece of fruit in half again to make 4 quarters **(fig. 2)**.

3. Cut up other pieces of fruit into fractions, including thirds, fourths, sixths, and eighths **(fig. 3)**.

4. Use toothpicks to create animals and other creatures from the fractioned fruit **(fig. 4)**.

5. What else could you create **(fig. 5)**?

CREATIVE ENRICHMENT

→ Look at the fruit you've cut in half and try to find symmetry. Use some of it to make fruit stamps (see Lab 36, page 100).

THE
STEAM
BEHIND THE FUN:

The Latin root for the word *fraction* means "to break." When you break an object into pieces, or cut it up, you create fractions.

A fraction is a number representing part of a whole thing, whether it's a number or an apple. If you cut an apple into two identical pieces and hold one piece in your hand, you are holding one of the two parts, or one-half of the whole apple. If you cut that piece in half again and hold it in your hand, you're holding one-fourth of the original apple. Cut that piece in half again and you're holding one-eighth of the apple, and so on.

The Ancient Greeks realized that if you cut something up enough times, eventually you'll end up with a piece too small to divide. They called this uncuttable piece an "atom," a term which we still use today to describe the smallest building blocks of matter.

STRING ART

SAFETY TIPS AND HINTS

→ Young children should have adult supervision around pushpins, which have sharp points and are a choking hazard.

→ Adult supervision is required when using a glue gun.

Make geometric shapes, beautiful patterns, and even colorful curves using a series of straight lines created by winding string around pins.

Fig. 3: Create a design by repeating patterns.

MATERIALS

→ Pushpins or toothpicks that have been cut in half
→ Cork or foam-core board
→ Ruler (optional)
→ Colorful string, yarn, or embroidery thread
→ Pipe cleaners
→ School glue or glue gun and glue sticks (optional)

PROTOCOL

1. Push the pushpins or toothpicks into cork or a foam-core board. Older kids can use a ruler to make them the same distance apart for more complicated designs (**fig. 1**).

2. Make a geometric shape or repeating pattern by wrapping string around one pin and then connecting it to other pins (**fig. 2**).

3. Create a design by repeating patterns (**fig. 3**).

4. Try using toothpicks and pipe cleaners to make shapes (**fig. 4**).

5. After completing your design, secure the string with glue (**fig. 5**).

Fig. 1: Put pushpins in to cork or foam-core board. Use a ruler to make them equal distances apart, if you like.

Fig. 2: Make shapes and patterns using a piece of string, thread, or yarn.

Fig. 4: Or use toothpicks instead of pins and make shapes using pipe cleaners.

Fig. 5: After wrapping the string around the pins, secure it with glue.

CREATIVE ENRICHMENT

→ Figure out how to create a parabolic curve using string art (see STEAM Behind the Fun following).

→ Engineer a frame that allows you to make three-dimensional geometric designs from string. Consider using wood and nails to build a sturdier frame.

THE
STEAM
BEHIND THE FUN:

An amazing number of shapes can be created using straight lines, like the ones you make when you stretch a string from one point to another. If you space pins evenly around a square, you can use them to make a grid from string.

Straight lines positioned in a certain way create a type of curved line, called a *parabolic curve*. This is the same type of curve the path of a ball makes when you throw it in the air.

To make a parabolic curve from string, position pins on perpendicular axes at equal distances apart. Then, connect a string from the X-axis pin closest to where the axes meet to a pin on the Y-axis that is farthest from the intersection. Connect the pin second closest to the first one (on the X-axis) to the pin second farthest away on the Y-axis and repeat the pattern several times to create a parabolic curve.

Malcolm
 Sarah
 Kyra
 Carissa
 Sean
 Ethan
 Elena

 Nora
 Harper
 Cece
 Cela
 Django
 Aurora
 Celestino

 Liam
Soren
Haakon
 Summer
 Arbel
 Rimon
 Carlo

 Enzo
 Divya
 Kirin
 John
Georgia
 Henry
Lauren

 Anna
 McKenna
 Zach
 Ella
Mason
 Ayla
Bridget

 Dylan
 Griffin
 Johanna
 Ana
 Zayna
 Maggie
 Khalil

Olivia   Sarah   May   Abigail   Avery   Scarlett   Jackson

Lakken   Claire   Isaac   Owen   Anna   Neva   Ellie

Eli   Simon

RESOURCES

THERE ARE MANY technology and art supply companies in brick and mortar locations. If you can't find what you need locally, these online retailers can help you out.

3V coin-cell batteries (Labs 11 and 17)
9V battery clip snap-on connectors (battery snaps) (Labs 12, 15, and 19)
AA battery holders (Labs 12, 15, and 19)
Low speed (rpm 100 or less) mini motor (Lab 12)
Mini electric motor for DIY toys (1500 rpm) (Labs 15 and 19)
Small alligator clip test leads (Labs 12, 15, 18, and 19)
Solar landscape path lights (Lab 13)
USA: www.amazon.com
Canada: www.amazon.ca
Europe: www.amazon.co.uk

Carrageenan and alum (Lab 31)
USA: www.hollanders.com and www.amazon.com
Canada: www.amazon.ca
Europe: www.amazon.co.uk

LEDs, basic 3mm and 5mm through-hole (Labs 11, 14, 15, 18, and 19)
USA: www.amazon.com
Canada: www.canadarobotix.com/led-lighting/parts-basic-led-green-5mm or www.amazon.ca
Europe: www.amazon.co.uk

Micro generator motor (Lab 18)
I recommend the Micro Motor Wind Turbine Generator DC Power DIY 0.1V-18V 200~6000rpm or CrocSee Micro 3 Phase AC Mini Hand Brushless Motor Generator Model Experiment Teaching Aid
USA: www.amazon.com
Canada: www.amazon.ca
Europe: www.amazon.co.uk

Sewable electronics (Lab 17)
USA: www.sparkfun.com/lilypad_sewable_electronics and www.adafruit.com
Canada: www.amazon.ca
Europe: www.amazon.co.uk

Skateboard bearings (Lab 4)
USA: www.zumiez.com/skate/bearings.html or www.amazon.com
Canada: www.bearingscanada.com/Skateboard-Bearings-s/2054.htm
Europe: www.sickboards.nl/en/33-bearings

ACKNOWLEDGEMENTS

WITHOUT MY FAMILY AND FRIENDS, this book wouldn't exist. Thank you especially to the following people:

→ My dad, Ron Lee, my physics (and history) advisor.

→ My mom, Jean Lee, who has always encouraged my love of the arts and puts up with endless conversations about science.

→ My husband, Ken, who spends his days in an office (and too many evenings and weekends working at home) so I can write about science.

→ My kids, Charlie, May, and Sarah, who support my science writing endeavors with creative ideas, humor, and patience.

→ My mother-in-law, Jan Heinecke, who has used art to inspire countless numbers of kids through her work with early childhood education and shares ideas with me.

→ Jonathan Simcosky, Renae Haines, David Martinell, Mary Ann Hall, and the design team at Quarry Books.

→ Amber Procaccini, who brings the joy of science to life in her photographs.

→ McKenna, who engineered the Disk Drop project (page 78), and Sarah, who invented the Homemade Disco Ball (page 38).

→ Jennifer, who let us invade her backyard for the sake of science.

→ Heather R.J. Fletcher and the Minnesota Center for Book Arts for the paper marbling inspiration.

→ The people at the Ax-Man surplus store in St. Louis Park, Minnesota, who told me how to make a bristle bot and helped me find a motor for the Wind Turbine project (page 52).

→ Pop-up book artist Matthew Reinhart, whose Science Friday video "Engineering the Perfect Pop" introduced me to pop-up folds.

→ The smart, funny, and beautiful kids whose smiles light up the pages of this book

ABOUT THE AUTHOR

LIZ HEINECKE has loved science since she was old enough to inspect her first caterpillar. After working in molecular biology research for ten years, she left the lab to kick off a new chapter in her life as a stay-at-home mom. Soon, she found herself sharing her love of science with her three kids and journaling their experiments and adventures on her Kitchen Pantry Scientist website.

These days, Liz appears regularly on television, makes science videos, and writes about science online and in books. Liz's work includes *Kitchen Science Lab for Kids*, *Outdoor Science Lab for Kids*, and *Star Wars Maker Lab*. When she's not driving her kids around and doing science outreach, you'll find Liz at home in Minnesota, singing, playing banjo, painting, running, and doing almost anything else to avoid housework.

Liz graduated from Luther College with an art major and a biology minor. She received her master's degree in bacteriology from the University of Wisconsin, Madison.

ABOUT THE PHOTOGRAPHER

AMBER PROCACCINI is a commercial and editorial photographer based in Minneapolis, Minnesota. She specializes in photographing kids, babies, food, and travel, and her passion for photography almost equals her passion for finding the perfect taco. Amber met Liz while photographing her first book, *Kitchen Science Lab for Kids*, and she knew they'd make a great team when they bonded over cornichons, pate, and brie. When Amber isn't photographing eye-rolling tweens or making cheeseburgers look sexy, she and her husband love to travel and enjoy new adventures together.

ABOUT MOUSE

MOUSE IS A NATIONAL YOUTH development nonprofit that believes in technology as a force for good. They empower all students to create with technology to solve real problems and make meaningful change in our world.

Mouse's web-based learning platform, Mouse Create, is designed for young people to build the skills they need to apply design and technology creatively to the world around them.

Mouse Create provides hands-on projects across the many areas of STEAM, including circuitry, coding, green technology, games, sewable tech, and more.

Mouse inspires young people to be the inventors, innovators, and creative problem solvers of the digital age. Visit their website at mouse.org to learn more.

INDEX

ALSO AVAILABLE

**Kitchen Science
Lab For Kids**
978-1-59253-925-3

**Outdoor Science
Lab For Kids**
978-1-63159-115-0

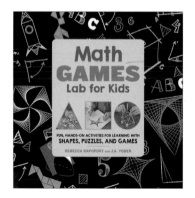

**Math Games
Lab For Kids**
978-1-63159-252-2

Art Lab For Kids
978-1-59253-765-5